Currently Classic

JONATHAN RACHMAN DESIGN

Flammarion

Currently Classic

JONATHAN RACHMAN DESIGN

TEXT
Dean Rhys Morgan

Flammarion

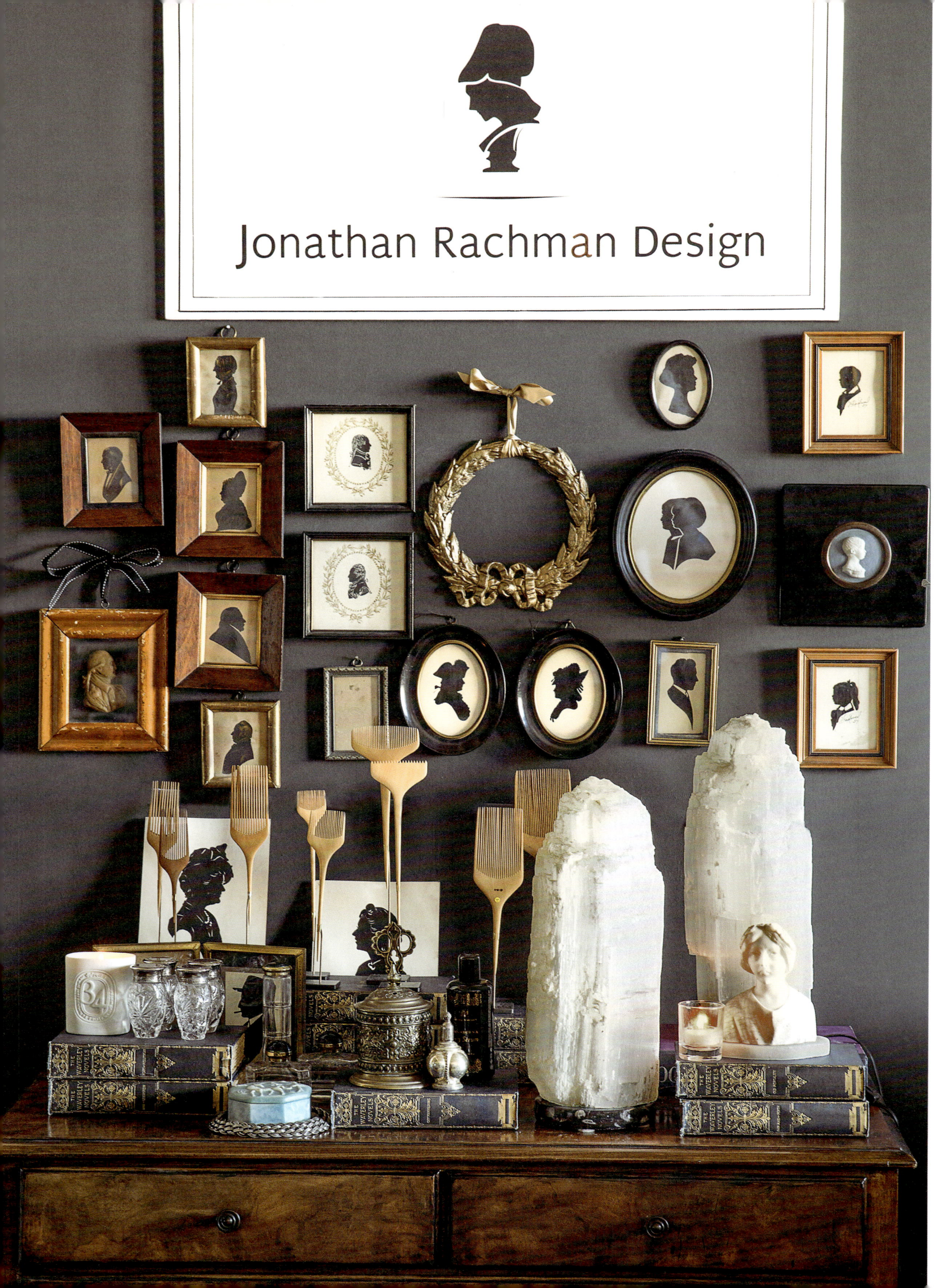

Jonathan Rachman Design

Contents

FACING PAGE
Collective spirit: an eclectic arrangement of Japanese hair combs, quartz table lamps, and silhouette portraits. Jonathan is a big fan of silhouettes, considering them both classic and timeless. His business card features a silhouette of Athena, goddess of handicraft and practical reason.

LEFT
A consummate collector, Jonathan surrounds himself with curios and personal mementos. Anything that might spark an idea, a design, or an exciting new color combination.

Foreword

DENISE HALE

I've always lived by my own set of rules. I do what I like—if you like it great; if not, I don't give a damn. It's a case of do or don't. I do like you or I don't like you. If I like you, I want to know you better.

Leafing through this beautiful book, I realize that almost seven years have passed since my first encounter with my darling Jonathan. What has made our friendship so rich? Jonathan and I share a sense of adventure, a desire to go places and to meet everybody. I've led a privileged life and had some fabulous houses. I've been incredibly fortunate to visit some of the world's most beautiful rooms. I can still recall Liliane de Rothschild's Paris mansion. I couldn't believe the beauty of it—to die for! I had never seen such beautiful rooms. The memory of her green salon stayed with me for years. Jonathan's rooms have had a similar effect. They make me want to linger, to absorb the details.

Jonathan's work has developed into an extension of his personality—it is warm, inviting, stylish, and luxurious. His rooms are filled with well-thought-out and original details, beautiful wallpapers, wonderful passementerie, and exquisite color combinations. Everything is carefully considered: furniture perfectly placed and magical pieces chosen to give his rooms that dash of daring. His imagination is like no other.

FACING PAGE
Mentor, muse, and confidante: Denise Hale, the internationally best-dressed doyenne of San Francisco shares Jonathan's passion for traditional craftsmanship and old-world charm. Portrait by Marc-Antoine Coulon.

Introduction

CLAUD CECIL GURNEY

One can always spot an interior by Jonathan Rachman. He uses all his experience gained in the magnificent past lives he's enjoyed in floral design, fashion, ballet, and architecture to curate every tiny detail so that nothing is forgotten. Open the desk drawer and the perfect scented notepaper will be waiting for you, together with a quill pen and purple ink. Creating beauty is Jonathan's art and, happily, he loves and adapts our products endlessly.

Jonathan is not just a social butterfly, although he performs that function to the delight of many people seamlessly and brilliantly; he is also a talented designer who adopts a holistic approach and flawlessly adapts his design to different clients and different circumstances. Whether it is a beach house in the South Pacific or an apartment in New York, he will always apply the same attention to detail, which ensures that the client is happy. One can always be sure that one will not only have a beautiful interior in keeping with one's taste and circumstances but also receive advice on how to set the table, how to stand for a photograph, how to take a selfie properly, how to arrange the flowers, which silver to use, and how to address Her Majesty the Queen when she comes to tea.

FACING PAGE
Claud Cecil Gurney and Jonathan photographed at the 2017 San Francisco Decorator Showcase. Behind them, a custom, hand-embroidered paper with the Silk Tree pattern, developed exclusively for Rachman's "A'musing In Paris" tableau.

PAGES 12–13
Pinterest: Souvenirs of the people, places, and objects that have inspired Jonathan over the course of his decorating life.

de Gournay
Johnathan Rachman,
1632C Market Street,
SAN FRANCISCO,
CA 94102,
USA

Spiced crème fraîche
A trio of local cheeses
Baron Bigod unpasteurised cows' milk brie
Mrs Temple's Binham Blue
Norfolk Dapple Cheddar
biscuits, fresh fruit
& homemade preserve
Locally roasted coffee &
fresh mint tea
chocolate truffles
& pistachio macarons
LEONE
PEPPERMINT
de Gournay
SHOWROOM
OPENING
I saw this and thought
of you so I had to get it
and send it to you...
xo
Margot

GUINNESS

A Creative Life

JONATHAN RACHMAN, IN CONVERSATION

Jonathan Rachman admires fashion designer Hubert de Givenchy for his timeless, elegant approach to design, Givenchy's one-time colleague Christian Dior for his romantic nostalgia, and stage designer Oliver Messel for his versatility, many talents, and adaptability. In a way, Rachman is the successor and sum of all his heroes and perhaps a touch more. From floral designs for Madonna and Marc Jacobs to party planning for the United Nations, he's done it all with aplomb, but the path for this multi-hyphenated creative was far from straightforward.

FACING PAGE
Mix master: Jonathan at his Market Street studio in San Francisco. He added the twenty-two-foot (6.7-m) wall of cabinetry, to display key pieces from his collection of vintage glass and porcelain. He painted the case Timber Wolf by Benjamin Moore.

FACING PAGE
Fresh and fascinating: "No room is complete without flowers," says Jonathan. English garden roses, hydrangeas—he has been arranging them since he was a child and insists they are always fresh and with the most intoxicating fragrances.

DEAN RHYS-MORGAN: What inspired you to get into design?

JONATHAN RACHMAN: Truly, I never planned to be an interior designer. I was your typical corporate soldier, and I certainly never studied design formally. My early education was in business and hospitality at Les Roches in Switzerland, but I learned quickly that I'd rather be a guest than an employee in a hotel or restaurant.

I always knew I was creative. As a kid, I drew and made silk flowers, but there was no light-bulb moment. I didn't follow the traditional path into the design business. I didn't work for anyone else. I didn't really have the tools to establish and build a business. All I had was a belief in myself. It was a happy accident. After graduation I got caught up in the repetitive nine-to-five world of corporate America. Big jobs, big titles, big responsibilities. I must have had over thirty positions in twelve years. I moved from non-profits to education and hospitality and back again. I was constantly looking for something that felt right and fit.

I was miserable. I hated corporate life, so I walked away and opened a flower shop. Fleur't was born in 2002. I rented a tiny space at a hair salon on Sacramento Street. It couldn't have been more than one hundred square feet. Again, I had no formal training—I just loved flowers. When I was growing up in Sumatra, I was surrounded by roses, and I used to help my mother arrange the flowers for church. Other than that, Fleur't was an entirely new proposition. It really was one of the most exuberant periods of my life; I loved every minute. The days were long and hard, but the business grew quickly through word of mouth. Fashion designer Marc Jacobs dropped by one afternoon and hired me to create arrangements for his flagship store on Maiden Lane. Then the Four Seasons appointed me their VIP florist, and I found myself creating bouquets for Madonna, Sarah Jessica Parker, and Oprah Winfrey. Soon I moved into event planning, and all the things that I had done instinctively since I was a kid—things that almost seemed to be part of my DNA—gradually became my life's work.

DRM: How did you get your first big assignment?

JR: I was flying to Paris via Frankfurt for Maison&Objet and found myself sitting next to an ambassador's wife, and we hit it off immediately. She was in the process of organizing the sixtieth anniversary party of the United Nations and, at thirty-eight thousand feet, she hired me to design and orchestrate the event and introduced me to Protocol Professionals Inc. It was a huge four-day extravaganza, with unprecedented levels of protocol and diplomacy. I took care of everything, from the floral arrangements and lighting to the food and décor. It took almost a year to pull together.

Gradually, the ladies who attended the events I designed began inviting me to decorate their homes. I explained that while I had no formal training, I thought I would be a good "fluffer." They laughed, I laughed, and I began fluffing their houses each week. Weeks turned into months, and months turned into years. Later, they asked me to design pieds-à-terre, summer homes, and beach houses. One project just followed another.

DRM: As a self-taught designer, was it difficult to find your own path in the design industry?

JR: It's not rocket science. I was always confident, I always said yes to opportunities as they arose, even if I had little or no experience in the field, and I always found a way to deliver what I had promised. I might not be your typical designer, but I had a definite voice. There is only so much you can learn theoretically. I get hired because I'm me. Half the job is chemistry; it always comes down to relationships. I have clients I have worked with on five consecutive houses, I've planned their weddings, and trimmed their Christmas trees. As someone once said, not all my friends are clients, but all my clients are friends.

FACING PAGE Jonathan opened his flower shop, Fleur't, on Sacramento Street, San Francisco, in 2002. His bold and unusual flower combinations quickly caused a sensation, and he soon began consulting with clients on the design of their homes, which led him to launch his own design firm. Marc-Antoine Coulon reimagines Rachman's flirty flowers.

DRM: What was your first experience of design?

JR: When my parents began building our house in Sumatra. It was a project that really introduced me to the idea of home. I was born and raised near the Krakatoa volcano, about 150–200 miles inland. Our hometown didn't even exist a hundred years ago because it was wiped out by a tsunami. My father was self-made. He came from nothing and became a success in the coffee and spice trade. He built our home in Sumatra from the ground up. Everything was custom. Indonesia has remarkable craftsmen, including one of the last skilled woodworkers to arrive in Sumatra from China. His craftsmanship was top of the line, and he created the most exquisite pagodas and latticework for our home. The house had an open courtyard and spread over four acres of land. The gardens were like the grounds of a hotel: manicured lawns, palm trees, koi fish. It left quite an impression.

DRM: How would you describe your style?

JR: I hope that I don't have a style. At least I don't try to project a style. I'd like to think that my work is current and classic; I don't follow trends. I'm not attempting to dilute someone else's message. My motto is to buy what you like because you will find a home for it. I don't like themes or trying too hard to achieve a particular look that somebody else has established. Rooms like that will never feel authentic. Surround yourself with souvenirs of your life, things that reflect your travels and passions.

DRM: Is there an essential element every room should have?

JR: Soul! In Europe there's a common thread in the best-designed homes. They may be very polished and pulled together, but they never feel staged. There's a sense of evolution and development. It's not so much about brands as it is about bringing together truly loved pieces, things that feel right. I want to inject a touch of the past into the present, to marry the old and the new, the expected and unexpected. Traces of the past add meaning and autobiography to a room. For a client, I might find old photographs of their region or vintage images of the family or a place they love. I like to bring emotion and soul to my interiors. The key is that they must be original, not copies, and they must have signs of life, of time passing. They are not necessarily precious, and sometimes they include furnishings that are chipped or faded—but I love flaws. Antiques take the design dialogue to another level.

DRM: How do you help clients navigate and express their own design aesthetic?

JR: As a designer you have to be a great listener. Tell me what you like, and I will show you who you are. It's something I say to all my clients. The best projects are invariably those where the client has a strong voice and distinctive point of view. My job is to translate their tastes and lifestyle into a home. I start by asking them what kind of story they want to tell, how they want it to feel. It's about evoking a mood. Designing is a form of storytelling, and while it's largely intuitive, there must be a synchronicity between beauty and practicality. Those characteristics work hand in hand; one does not have to exclude the other.

DRM: What makes a room feel good to you as soon as you walk in?

JR: Knowing that someone actually uses it. There's a big difference between a beautiful room and a room you really want to live in. You can immediately tell the difference between a room that's used versus one that's never entered; there's a certain warmth about it. I always caution clients that you have to own your house; the house doesn't own you.

Fleur*t

FACING PAGE
Paper with a past: A detail of de Gournay's Saint Laurent wallpaper, a design inspired by a set of panels belonging to couturier Yves Saint Laurent. The provenance of the papers is as dazzling as the design. Famed American decorator Syrie Maugham sold them to socialite Mona Harrison Williams in the 1930s. They then passed into the hands of collector and connoisseur Jayne Wrightsman.

DRM: How do you work? How do you transform your client's vision into reality?

JR: If you establish a good furniture plan when you start, you're going to buy things in the right scale. I'm very hands on, I like to get out and look at things. I'm not the kind of designer who puts together a scheme and has a few client meetings. You have to be an advocate for your ideas. You have to do things well and put in the work or there's a danger that everything can turn into the same thing. I see too many rooms that are almost paint-by-number. Each project has to have its own identity. Once the functional, practical elements have been established, the fun begins—selecting decorative finishes, and colors.

DRM: You have a great love of color. How do you go about gathering colors and creating palettes?

JR: Have a reference point. Find something that you love, like a painting or wallpaper, or a pattern, and build from that. Experimenting with color combinations can bring out unexpected magic. A monochromatic décor does not have to be pale. Play with different combinations of hue, brightness, and saturation. Colors like cobalt blue, kelly green, or eggplant can evoke the monochromatic in a daring way, one that's full of personality and elegance.

DRM: Let's talk about wallpaper, particularly your collaborations with Hannah Cecil Gurney of de Gournay. That firm's wallcoverings have become a staple of your design work.

JR: People have become less afraid of wallpaper over the last few years. It's had a bad rap, particularly among younger clients. I've always been crazy for wallpaper, and de Gournay has long been my go-to. They bring a fresh, modern twist to classically inspired designs, and the attention to detail is unparalleled. I don't think people realize that everything made by de Gournay is hand-painted. If you look closely, you can see pencil marks and individual brushstrokes. It's not something you can duplicate with a machine.

DRM: Can we talk about scale? Scale is an interesting and difficult topic, particularly for a self-taught designer. How do you achieve a good scale?

JR: Scale, texture, and color are my holy trinity. But part of the benefit of never having had a formal design education is that I break all kinds of rules, because I have never learned what the rules are. There are some parameters of acceptable scale for a space. That being said, I don t subscribe to smaller-scale furnishings for a smaller room. In fact, at times, when it's appropriate, I do just the opposite. A larger object or piece of furniture in a smaller space can create a visual illusion for greater impact. Scale can be very subjective.

DRM: Any pet peeves?

JR: I can't have time for fake flowers, no silk or plastic; they collect nothing but dust. A room without fresh flowers is like a fashionably dressed lady without any jewelry. Flowers are the icing on the cake, they complete the look of the space.

DRM: How does fashion influence your own design work?

JR: My first passion in design was fashion. In fact, my graduate study was in dress: I was mentored by the brilliant fashion artist Gladys Perint Palmer, and the fashion designer Alexander McQueen invited me to intern with him. Hubert de Givenchy and Christian Dior have always spoken to my aesthetic. They are both current and classic, their designs as captivating and romantic today as they were originally. Oliver Messel also inspires me, he's such a chameleon. He could turn his hand to anything: theater, film, architecture, interior design.

RIGHT
Balinese woodwork from Ubud. "The patterns and patina are impossible to ignore," says Jonathan.

FACING PAGE
A view of a Stupa of the Borobudur Temple near Jonathan's father's village and his favorite home away from home: the Amanjiwo.

Each time I discover something that catches my eye, I take a quick photo. I'm always looking for unusual patterns and details, I have almost 300,000 images filed away on my iPhone at this point. It's almost like a reference library.

WIC
BEDROOM 3

FACING PAGE
Pattern powerhouse: For his "Ashbury Heights" design Jonathan pulled together multiple fabric and passementerie samples.

My friend Denise Hale has become a direct link to this golden age of couture. She was a close friend and client of Givenchy and knew Messel socially. She's become something of a muse and mentor. She appreciates old school charm and craftsmanship. In a flighty world, she's refreshingly loyal. If Denise decides you're her friend, her support is unwavering; I can't imagine a world without her. In a sea of fake diamonds, reality television shows, and housewives of every major city, Denise is the real deal.

DRM: Are you familiar with the Oliver Messel Suite at the Dorchester hotel?

JR: It's pure fantasy, almost like being in a film set: the buttercup-yellow silk, the chintz, the painted doors, the rococo fountain. Like Oliver Messel, I'm a bit of a maximalist. Too much is never enough!

DRM: What are your inspirations?

JR: Travel is the biggest. It's a love I inherited from my dad, and it's been my greatest design education. Travel hones the eye and broadens the mind. The more informed you become, the greater your creative vocabulary. I've circled the globe more times than I count. I often invite clients to travel with me to shop. When we travel, we look at things differently. Clients can relax and relay their likes and dislikes more casually; this helps me collect pieces with them rather than for them. There's a shared history.

DRM: You pull a lot of your inspiration from these trips. How do you describe your travel style?

JR: I'm a neurotic traveler. I make it a point to be considerate of others by keeping my look chic yet comfy. I remember in the 1970s, people still dressed up to travel. I like to change into my pajamas on a long flight. I like proper linen and china while I am enjoying my inflight meal. I'm also obsessed with the idea of creating the perfect leather travel bag, done the old-fashioned way, from Italy. My parents always had proper carry-on and weekend bags, I can still remember the way they were lined and smelled. There's something incredibly special about having a signature leather bag.

DRM: How do you document your inspirations, particularly when traveling? Do you sketch, take photographs?

JR: My iPhone is invaluable. I don't sketch, but I might discover a door with beautiful paneling on it, so I will take a few shots. Each time I discover something that catches my eye, I take a quick photo. I'm always looking for unusual patterns and details, I have almost 300,000 images filed away on my iPhone at this point. It's almost like a reference library. I've also enlarged images and placed them in rooms for clients. A collector's library I designed included one of my own photos: a gorgeous sunset taken from the window seat of an Airbus 330. The piece was purchased, with the proceeds benefiting a Balinese school in need.

DRM: Travel also fuels your own passion for collecting.

JR: I collect, collect, collect. Everywhere I go, I find something I can't live without. I'm an emotional collector. I like old things inspired by childhood memories. I like to preserve and share. I'm obsessed with typography, letters, and calligraphy. I rarely pass up a pretty "J." I've been storing things for decades with the hope of one day being able to tell some kind of story with it all. And, voilà, in 2015 I found a space on Market Street and opened J. Rachman, the store. I'd had a crush on the building for years. Formerly a piano shop, it was built in 1911. It's such a romantic space and always reminded me of Paris. I wanted to give San Francisco the kind of atelier you'd discover on a quiet street in the Marais or London, a shop full of curiosities, where you can browse and touch things that might be hundreds of years old. San Francisco didn't need another mid-century-modern shop or a store full of faux industrial reproductions. The store is my play space.

FACING PAGE
A passion for pattern: Traditional hand-painted Balinese umbrellas in Ubud's artist village. "The bold, bright colors and patterns are stunning, yet they blend into the natural surroundings," says Jonathan.

RIGHT
Quiet beauty: Pura Masceti, one of Bali's lesser-known temples. According to legend, the god Wisnu and Laksmi, the goddess of wealth and prosperity, would have long discussions here while admiring the scenery.

I rediscovered Asia in my late 20s, when I started going back to Indonesia. I was absolutely in love. It's a constant source of inspiration.

The building had wonderful bones, and I held onto the original hardwood floors. I also kept the sheet music that was wallpapered to the ceiling, between the exposed beams. My mom was a church pianist, and it seemed like a fitting tribute. My only addition was a twenty-two-foot wall of built-ins and the creation of a design studio on the mezzanine. I want people to come in, take a look around, and be inspired—even if the only thing they take home with them is a good idea.

DRM: What made you decide to set up in San Francisco?

JR: I came to America as a foreign exchange student and, for me, San Francisco really was love at first sight. As much as it's an established city, it's constantly shifting and evolving. It's classic yet current, and the perfect distillation of my style: it's East-West, it's an old-new or a new-old city; it's a big-small city and a small-big city. There's an Indonesian expression, *Di Sini Di Sana*, that translates as "here and there." I sometimes feel caught between two worlds. I live in and love the West, but my heart is often pulled East, toward my family and roots.

DRM: *Di Sini Di Sana* also became the name and message of your in-house magazine.

JR: The magazine is my love letter to both worlds, a chance to share the best of what is here (in the West) and the best of what is there (in the Far East). As a designer, I feel I am that much more advanced as a result of the Eastern and Western influences. That combination makes me more versatile in what I do. For me, both worlds embody the perfect harmony and balance, sort of the yin and yang. One affects the other. On a personal level, the East and the West are basically me: as an individual, as a human, as a designer. I am the product of the East, where I was born and raised up to a certain point, while the West is where I have spent most of my life. My love for both worlds is a natural progression in my life, since both worlds have given me so many gifts in foundations, experiences, beauty, and, more importantly, family.

DRM: Why a traditional printed magazine in the digital age. I know you love digital communication and Instagram.

JR: I'm a romantic. I believe in the beauty of timeless design. Some things never go out of style: a handsome wingback chair, a weathered leather satchel, an alabaster lamp, a vase full of French tulips. The same goes for an old-fashioned letter, the kind you put a stamp on. In this world of email, texts, blogs, and Pinterest, I still believe in the beauty of tangible things. I love to go to my mailbox and receive a thank-you note from someone who took the time to put pen to paper. We live in a world of iPads and Kindles, and yet, I'm a designer who still relishes sitting down with a glass of wine and a beautifully printed book, or a martini and my favorite magazine. I love the art of holding something meaningful in my hands and perusing it at leisure, without the glow of a screen, or the call of a keyboard. I want to turn pages with my fingertips and see photographs and beautiful fonts under the ambient light of a lamp. With all that in mind, I decided to create my own response to the modern-day blog. A newsletter with the emphasis on "letter." I'm writing a design missive, a small book of my thoughts on design, travel, food, and drink, told in the general stream of consciousness that comes with a conversation between two old friends. People love a story. In Hawaii, the aunties consider storytelling an art form. They call it "talk story," a phrase that resonates with me in all walks of life; stories—from the origins of some of my favorite design elements to the ingredients of my favorite cocktails. It's a chance to discuss projects, talk about my favorite sources of beautiful textiles and furnishings, share anecdotes and pictures from my travels, and give people a look inside my endless stream of inspiration.

DRM: But you go back. I know Bali has become a personal touchstone and point of inspiration.

JR: I rediscovered Asia in my late 20s, when I started going back to Indonesia. I was absolutely in love. Especially Bali and Java; Bali has actually become my second home. I try to spend part of every year on the island, and I'm in the process of building a home there. It's so rich culturally, and my family has been visiting since the early 1960s. It's a constant source of inspiration. I've spent many months there with my parents, traveling to different parts of the island.

DRM: What has been the best thing about starting your own business?

JR: Freedom on so many different levels-time, aesthetics, imagination for example. And there is no predetermined limit to what you can or want to achieve.

DRM: What's next? Is there a dream project?

JR: It would be wonderful to overhaul an airline, everything from the airline interior, to the cabin, lounge, branding, and uniforms. The amount of time I spend in and out of airports is astronomical. I love to collaborate, but I'm more interested in organic partnerships with artisans than stamping my name on products. I've developed two lines of textiles with Ellis Dunn, both very personal and autobiographical. The Sisters Collection was an homage to the women in my life; the mothers, sisters and friends who have helped raise, sustain, and lift me. The Brothers Collection is a tribute to the male figures in my life and what it means to be a man-a gentle man. The design influences, like the subjects, were a mix of both East and West, Balinese meets the Left Bank. I just want to continue doing what I love best: designing and travelling, growing my clientele internationally. BIKA Living have invited me to create a line of furniture and home accessories. I have been commissioned to design a boutique hotel in Scotland, a place in Europe and a few major projects locally and nationally.

On a personal level, I want to travel more than ever and spend quality time with my loved ones. My parents are getting older and I miss them dreadfully, as my husband Stephen says "eternity is too short and eternity is not long enough!"

I'm a romantic. I believe in the beauty of timeless design. Some things never go out of style: a handsome wingback chair, a weathered leather satchel, an alabaster lamp, a vase full of French tulips.

C3
23
C1
C3
17

Interiors

Christian Dior felt living in a house that doesn't reflect who you are was like wearing someone else's clothes. It's a sentiment shared by Jonathan Rachman; part of Jonathan's magic is his ability to create spaces that reflect the personalities of each of his clients. He's adopted Monsieur Dior's philosophy and carried it over into the way he approaches home design, seamlessly translating clients' likes and tastes into a home. "There's such a similarity between the clothes we choose to wear and the objects we choose to surround ourselves with. In fashion there is Haute Couture, ready-to-wear, etcetera. I apply that concept to design. I dress rooms the way my clients dress themselves. Some rooms should be formal, others should be casual and comfortable. Each project has to have its own identity."

FACING PAGE
Thinking decoratively: "Houghton Reimagined" mood board for the 2019 San Francisco Decorator Showcase. For Jonathan, design is a form of storytelling. For each project he pulls together dozens of images and samples. They allow him to create a coherent design concept without losing sight of his client's likes and objectives.

OLIVER MESSEL
A KIND OF WOMAN
INTERIORS
CHARLOTTE MOSS DECORATES
SYRIE MAUGHAM

Houghton Reimagined

SAN FRANCISCO DECORATOR SHOWCASE HOUSE

"Among the many amazing women in my life is Lady Rose Hanbury, a muse and a dear friend," says Rachman of the English aristocrat known formally as the Marchioness of Cholmondeley. It was her home at Houghton Hall in Norfolk, in the east of England, that inspired the designer's scheme for the showhouse's entertainment room. On a visit to the eighteenth-century estate several years ago, Rachman had the opportunity to view antique chinoiserie wallpaper panels that had been long lost in the attics of Houghton. Safe from light and heat, the panels retained their original, vibrant colors, and left a lasting impression on the designer, who knew the day would come when he could put de Gournay's impeccable reproduction of the Houghton paper to use. The showhouse proved the perfect opportunity. Rachman, who weaves a narrative for every showcase project, imagined the room as a place where the family and a few close friends could retreat—still in their finery—after the conclusion of a formal State dinner. The resulting room is a dramatic space, wrapped in the striking, blue floral wallpaper. A grand, fifteen-foot (4.5-m) canapé sofa was upholstered in a bright pink silk, the color picked up in the drapery panels and again echoed in the berry-red of the banquette. Decorative accents fill the space ("When it comes to accessories, more is never enough," says Rachman), including portraits of the family, antiques, urns, neoclassical busts—even a taxidermy pheasant. To the side of the main room, Rachman fitted a small, jewel-toned chamber with a pair of French Empire daybeds—a luxurious retreat within a retreat. "Be creative with the use of furniture," pleads the designer. "Don't be limited simply by the title of the room. A small room can be a reading nook, somewhere to take a nap, or a place to have afternoon tea or a cocktail if you're imaginative with the furnishings."

FACING PAGE
Layers of loveliness: Inspired by England's historic Houghton Hall, Jonathan's living room is a maximalist homage to the art and craft of Claud Cecil Gurney. To bring his grand reinvention to life he drew heavily upon de Gournay's silk damask fabrics, Chippendale-style mirrors, and a custom China blue colorway of their hand-painted Houghton wallpaper. The result: chinoiserie at its finest.

PAGES 34-35
Given the scale of the room, Jonathan's first objective was to make it feel less intimidating. To achieve this, he placed a large sofa opposite the fireplace. Dior inspired and upholstered with bright rose satin from de Gournay; it sets the tone for the entire room. A velvet ottoman christened "Lady R" is flanked by four chartreuse Coup d'État bucket chairs, transforming the seating area into an intimate conversation spot.

ART
FLYING
ART OF FL

FACING PAGE
To distinguish what Jonathan describes as "the jewel box room" from the main seating area, he painted the space a dazzling cobalt blue and installed a twinkling Lobmeyer Sputnik chandelier. The result is an elegant sleeping nook, the vibrant blue providing a touch of drama and contrast that lends a sense of ease to the main room.

RIGHT *Houghton Revisited* by Marc-Antoine Coulon.

PAGES 38–39
Lex Pott's Tree of Light chandelier hangs from a painted starry night sky, a scene that echoes the lighthearted whimsy of the de Gournay wallpaper.

MLINARIC ON DECORATING

PAGES 40–41
Pretty passementerie: Jonathan delights in trims. Tufts of horsehair cascade from Thing, a bespoke round ottoman by Coup Studio covered in Designers Guild's Pavia Essentials fabric. The orange Casablanca base fringe from Décor de Paris adds a pop of color to a bespoke velvet banquette.

FACING PAGE
Moss green woodwork is given an extra spark of elegance with accents of traditional water-gilding.

RIGHT
Portrait of a lady: Rose Cholmondeley, the current chatelaine of Houghton, photographed by Agnes Lloyd-Platt. To the left of her portrait is a porcelain lighting sconce by Boatswain.

LEFT
Styled to the max: When it comes to accessories, more is never enough for Jonathan. He loves to stack books, flowers, and decorative objects on surfaces to create a bold silhouette. "Besides being visually pleasing and chic, you still have room for your cocktails and aperitifs," he says. "Remember, clusters prevent clutter!"

FACING PAGE
Jonathan's exuberant mixing of color and pattern is tempered by subtler design choices, such as the dark wood credenza.

Russian Hill Chic

Mary Beth Shimmon is a true original, a globe-trotting front-row fashion personality whose passion for design and the decorative arts translates eloquently into the Russian Hill home she shares with her husband, David. "I've always been crazy about Jonathan and his work," says Shimmon. "We both view art and design as a means of self-expression, and we have a lot of the same sensibilities." Bowled over by Rachman's "A'musing In Paris" tribute to Audrey Hepburn at the San Francisco Decorator Showcase, Shimmon and Rachman quickly struck up a friendship. "San Francisco is a small town," reflects Shimmon, "so when you find a friend on a similar wavelength, you stick together!"

An exhibit of paintings by Jeremiah Goodman at Rachman's design studio was the starting point for their first design collaboration. "I was obsessed with a painting of Carolina Herrera's drawing room," remembers Shimmon. "It was so dramatic and color-saturated. It happens that I've been wearing a lot of very strong pieces by Wes Gordon for Carolina Herrera the past few years. We took that as a sign and drew our inspiration for the room from the painting. Of course, we included Mr. Goodman's piece in the room," she explains.

Further cues for the home's design were taken from another fashion icon, Pauline de Rothschild. In the late 1960s, *Vogue* commissioned Horst P. Horst to photograph the baroness at her hôtel particulier on Rue Méchain, the walls of which were wrapped in a panorama of hand-painted eighteenth-century chinoiserie wallpaper. While the original panels vanished after her death, her *salon vert* became a point of reference for decades. In 2017, de Gournay released an interpretation of the design, with pheasants, sparrows, parakeets, and a magpie nestled amongst the foliage and butterflies. Shimmon and Rachman were smitten, but shook things up by commissioning a custom colorway from de Gournay—in, what else, but shocking pink! It's another inspired nod to a fashion heroine: surrealist couturier Elsa Schiaparelli. There are Hollywood connections, too. The bar used to belong to Lauren Bacall and Humphrey Bogart. "To me, Mary Beth and David are the Bogie and Bacall of our time," says Rachman. "Chic, elegant, iconic."

FACING PAGE
The chicest of living rooms: René Bouché's 1959 portrait of model China Machado hangs on a custom shocking-pink colorway of de Gournay's Salon Vert chinoiserie wallpaper. The floor-to-ceiling windows are dressed in a combination of de Gournay, Manuel Canovas, and Kravet fabrics, with passementerie by Décor de Paris. The chaise was picked up at Chairish and lacquered a rich ebony.

RIGHT
A bronze and crystal chandelier by Baccarat hangs above a bespoke dining table designed by Jonathan, while an abstract canvas by Santiago Parra sits between a pair of eighteenth-century grisaille paintings. The sconces are Italian neoclassical.

FACING PAGE
The hallway is home to a vintage Versace chair from the boutique on Rodeo Drive which sits beneath an Iva sconce by Aerin Lauder. The wall covering is Sotatsu Spring by Anna Glover.

LEFT
A view of the breakfast room, featuring a group of cast-bronze Amsterdam chairs by Magni Home Collection.

BELOW
A dash of daring: To update a vintage luggage trolley Jonathan added fresh upholstery. He chose Jokhang Tiger velvet by Johnson Hartig for Schumacher.

ABOVE
Jonathan describes the Shimmons as the Bogart and Bacall of Russian Hill—how fitting, therefore, that Bogie's wet bar has found its way to their living room. Above the bar hangs a watercolor by interior portraitist Jeremiah Goodman. The abstract canvas is by American graffiti artist Retna. The Grotto chair is Venetian gilt wood.

FACING PAGE
Russian Hill by Marc-Antoine Coulon.

PAGES 54–55
Symmetry: Two identical Lucite chandeliers hang at opposites ends of the living room. To the right, above the wet bar, hangs the watercolor of Carolina Herrera's drawing room from which the Shimmons and Jonathan drew their inspiration for the room's overhaul. The seating plan is completed by a pair of faux bamboo armchairs that flank a bespoke tufted sofa by Coup Studio. The Toile de Jouy elephant is by Christian Dior.

FRANÇOIS CATROUX
SULTAN

CLEVELAND
ZOO

A Mansion with a View

"I wanted to honor the historical façade of this house while bringing it into this century with luxury, warmth, and much-needed intimacy," Rachman explains of this monumental project, a 24,000-square-foot (2,230-m^2), five-story landmark residence on the southeast corner of the Presidio, San Francisco's most famous park. When Rachman was commissioned to design not only the interior of the 1905 home, but also the exterior, as well as its suspended courtyard, he said yes right away and immediately presented the owners with a portfolio of architectural inspirations and details. Perched high enough to enjoy picture-postcard views of the Golden Gate Bridge, this project was a culmination of Rachman's classic-meets-current approach to design.

There are all his signature details—comfortable (and plentiful) seating, fine antiques, chinoiserie, portrait silhouettes—as well as his playful spirit, so wonderfully distilled in the living room's coral-hued consoles. Besides traveling worldwide, collecting, and proposing his finds to the clients, he was involved in every aspect of creating this exceptional home, from inception through to final flourishes. (He has even designed floral arrangements for the owners' lavish parties.) With formal reception rooms, which include an art gallery and a thirty-seat dining room, multiple kitchens, a wine lounge, his and hers offices, nine bedrooms and fifteen baths, an artist's studio, a twenty-five-car garage, a basketball court, a guest house, and nanny's quarters, plus countless other luxury features, it isn't surprising that Rachman and his team have devoted over a decade to its design. "It has been a sometimes-challenging project," the designer admits, "but it has been rewarding. I am truly honored to have contributed to the history of this magnificent house." And he couldn't have been more pleased than to hear the client's kind words when he paid a visit to the designer's 2019 showcase house. "He told me, 'I always knew you would be exactly where you are, as cream rises to the top.'"

FACING PAGE
In the homeowner's study, a parcel-gilt chandelier frames the double doorway, offering a glimpse of the dining room beyond. Jonathan used a custom blend of Black Forest and Mossy Green paint by Benjamin Moore to wash the boiserie a delicate green, accenting details with touches of water gilding. To furnish the room he chose a pair of traditional Chesterfield sofas and an English partner's desk. On the walls he hung a collection of *Vanity Fair* illustrations.

ABOVE AND FACING PAGE
The idyllic outdoor seating area features a suite of furniture from Brown Jordan in Formation fabric, creating a calm space for relaxing after a long day.

PAGES 60–61
In the living room Jonathan covered a pair of vintage kidney-shaped sofas in chinoiserie silk. For the curtains he chose Sanderson's Pagoda River, an early design from the Eton Rural Collection of the 1910s. To illuminate the room, he chose a coronet-topped French pendant light.

ABOVE
In an example of his skill at creating rooms that are both timeless and elegant, Jonathan furnished this room with a combination of his own bespoke furniture designs and a collection of vintage and antique pieces.

FACING PAGE
In the entrance hall a Regency giltwood mirror hangs above an Italian carved-wood console.

PAGES 64–65
Jonathan gave the wet bar the feel of a traditional gentlemen's club. He covered the bespoke walnut bar in tufted leather. The bar stools are vintage and covered with Stroheim fabric. To the right hangs a photograph by British installation artist Isaac Julien, *Pas de Deux 2*, from his 1989 film, *Looking for Langston*.

NAPOLEON
10¢ CIGAR

FACING PAGE
Jonathan enlivened the second-floor landing with Psyche Au Bain, a wallpaper mural by Zuber. Flanking the mural are a pair of gilt tole lanterns.

ABOVE
A beautifully made bronze and copper lantern hangs above the sweeping walnut staircase. To outfit the stairs Jonathan chose a Stark carpet.

ABOVE AND FACING PAGE
The kitchen features bespoke colored cabinetry with Calacatta marble countertops. Although heavily veined, the marble feels calm and combines elegantly with the cabinetry and walnut floors. The Pelham light pendants in polished nickel are by Hudson Lighting.

PAGES 70–71
In the bedroom, crisp neutral walls are given an instant lift with an abundant mix of textiles. A mid-century Auburn chandelier lights the room.

MARUCA GOMEZ
MONK OF MOKHA
A GENTLEMAN IN MOSCOW

"Heroine" Chic

SAN FRANCISCO DECORATOR SHOWCASE HOUSE

"Gold and champagne rule this room!" Rachman exclaims of his glittering design for the showcase home's foyer and stairway. The designer took inspiration from fashion icon Kate Moss's signature "heroin chic" style of the 1990s, and then added in a more contemporary spirit with additional influences from Lorde's 2013 song "Royals," about wealth, success, and the good life. With those touchstones in mind, the designer crafted a shimmering space grounded by a hide rug splatter-painted with gold and anchored by a contemporary, leather-upholstered tête-à-tête that invites lounging—and perhaps whispered conversations. The designer commissioned artists Hanh and Caroline Lizarraga to recreate Moss's likeness in a series of unique works for the space. Hanh conceived a mixed media installation that snakes up the skylit stairway, while Lizarraga applied Moss's profile to a mirror hung above a giltwood Georgian console. References to the fashion world come both subtly, as in the Missoni-like pattern of the metallic stair runner, and dramatically, with two antique, iron dressmaker forms and an extraordinary Indonesian headdress of golden flowers artfully displayed in a corner. Rachman perfumed the space with white roses—Moss's favorite flower. It's an interior marked by hushed luxury and high fashion—and femininity. Rachman playfully refers to the room's aesthetic as "heroine" chic, to acknowledge his respect for the creative work of his muses, Moss and Lorde. His design would no doubt have pleased the model, who has claimed a love of "mixing old and new things, all different eras." While the space is utterly glamorous and downright decadent, Rachman also used his magic to imbue it with an intangible spirit of rebellion, which Moss, who has said she hopes to be a rock star in her next lifetime, would surely embrace.

FACING PAGE
All about Kate: As befitting the woman who inspired it, this is a room for grand entrances and exits. Jonathan anchored the space with a crosshatch chandelier by Ironies. The area rug by Vaheed Taheri is a hand-sewn couture cowhide with metallic gold accents.

RIGHT
Tête-à-tête: A bespoke sectional sofa covered in Venice leather by S.H. Frank & Company—the perfect spot for cocktails and glamour.

FACING PAGE
At the foot of the staircase Jonathan posed two vintage dressmaker's forms picked up in Paris. The bridal headdress is antique and was discovered on a trip to Sumatra.

PAGES 76–77
Glittering reflections: A wraparound collage of Moss by Hahn has been applied to a series of smoked champagne mirrors. The installation snakes up the staircase.

FACING PAGE
Jonathan customized Donghia's Duca mirror with the instantly recognizable profile of Moss.

LEFT
A Flint lamp by Castel sits atop a Carrara marble-topped console.

Downtown Luxury

For a San Francisco high-rise home with extraordinary views of the Bay Bridge, Rachman knew to embrace the view, not fight it. On sunny days, when the water is a brilliant blue and the city bustles below, the home, done primarily in soft gray tones, lets those clear vistas create the "wow" factor. But on foggy days, certainly the norm for the city, the room is less about the view and more about softened light and feeling at one with the environment—cloudlike, quiet, and serene. It's a uniquely San Francisco atmosphere, one that even captured the imagination of John Lennon, who said during one visit with Yoko, "We've never been in a city with light like this. We sit in our hotel room for hours, watching the fog come in, the light change." In this home, neutral tones flourish, enhanced by contemporary artworks and the occasional moment of color, like the dining room chairs that Rachman did in chartreuse and fuchsia. In the living room, a curving platform sofa lounges in a glazed corner, the perfect perch from which to take in the surroundings, and that ever-changing sky. The designer opted for simple materials—glass, metal, leather ("I'm obsessed with fine leathers," he quips), unfinished or dark-stained woods—adding luxurious rugs and textiles to the mix. Most eschew pattern, but there are lively moments, too, with geometric, David Hicks-inspired prints on pillows. Subtle details abound, too, like the nail-head trim on a desk chair or the unexpected silver finish of a chandelier. In the bedroom, Rachman further softened the palette by shifting into whites, creams, and mossy greens. Velvet fabrics add texture, while lacquered furnishings add a sleek and contemporary note, all in keeping with the home's refined simplicity. "I let San Francisco—the city itself—be the inspiration," he says.

FACING PAGE
On the wall, *Annabelle H*, a backlit shadowbox by German artist Florian Schneider. The dining chairs are covered in Aurelia by Designers Guild in chartreuse and fuchsia.

PAGES 82–83
Minimal and modern: A handblown glass chandelier by Donghia hangs above a bespoke daybed upholstered in Janus & Cie fabric. For the bolster cushion, Jonathan chose French linen, while the cushions are covered in David Hicks and Cole & Son's fabrics. The multi-armed candelabra is by Anthem.

ABOVE
Inviting seating and low lighting have been used to create welcoming zones in the room. The C table is from Arden home.

FACING PAGE
Hand-painted: An industrial metal cabinet has been painted with the Manhattan skyline.

PAGES 86–87
On the wall, a painting by Russian artist Konstantin Bessmertny. To the right of the canvas is a Garbo daybed from Holly Hunt. The driftwood coffee table is by Big Daddy.

SICRET INTELIGENT SERVISE
HEROES OF
COLD WAR
MI5. MI6. KГБ. ФСБ. CIA. FBI
MOSSAD

FACING PAGE
A cowhide catchall holds an arrangement of viburnum, artichokes, and cymbidium orchids by Jonathan.

ABOVE
An arrangement of dried snowberries sits beside a marble bowl from a French flea market.

A Weekend Cottage

Nowhere is Rachman's sense of charm more at play than in a wine-country home he created for a family. The house is filled with all the traditional country elements one might expect to find, from an antique hutch laden with earthenware dishes, Wedgwood, silver objects, and books on French style to a true farmhouse kitchen with a center island designed for entertaining. But Rachman has also played with what a house in the country can be. There are whimsical moments—the breakfast nook's metal chairs adorned with birds and rabbits, the giant apple sculpture on the coffee table—but there are also sophisticated, old-world aspects, and the occasional surprise. For the dining room, the designer gave white-painted Louis XVI chairs an edge with inky-blue leather upholstery, while in the living room, he added a French Empire settee covered in a pale lilac fabric on the front and an unexpected toile on back. Historic design elements continue in the bedrooms, one of which features a Victorian brass headboard and a set of framed neoclassical-style intaglios. Another bedroom was given a luxurious, silk-upholstered headboard accented with silvered nail-head trim, but Rachman added an edgy twist to the space with embossed crocodile-print pillows and black lampshades. For the children's room, a purple-hued retreat for two little ones, the designer created dramatically arched twin headboards, each topped with a cherub, and dressed the beds with polka-dot linens. Throughout the home are bay windows that Rachman turned into cozy reading nooks, replete with soft blankets. "Splurge on good cashmere blankets or throws," he advises. "They last a long time." To knock back the hot afternoon sun but keep the views plentiful, the designer opted for Roman shades, choosing an array of prints, from damask and stripes to florals.

FACING PAGE
On the wall, a Dutch colonial display-case holds a small collection of ceramics discovered in Bali. The bespoke sofa sits alongside a painted Italian console and side table.

PAGES 92–93
In the dining room, a bespoke table by Bika Living. The chairs are in the Louis XVI style and were discovered at St. Ouen flea market in Paris; they retain their original inky-blue leather cushions.

RIGHT
The homeowner's collection of porcelain is displayed in a vintage glass-fronted Italian cabinet.

FACING PAGE
The table in the breakfast nook began life as a vase Jonathan picked up in Bologna; he added a base and hexagonal lid in Carrara marble to complement the kitchen island. The window-seat cushion is baseball-stitched boar hide.

PAGES 96–97
The simple metro wall tiles tie in with the bistro-style lighting. Three polished nickel Pelham shades by Hudson Valley Lighting hang above a custom Carrara marble island.

FACING PAGE
A Victorian bell jar from J. Rachman Design displays architectural elements from the client's collection.

ABOVE
In the living room, Jonathan paired a carved French-style sofa with a mercury-glass coffee table. The poufs are by Jennifer Robbins.

ABOVE
A simple flower arrangement by Jonathan rests on a bespoke window-seat cushion in Schumacher fabric.

FACING PAGE
A bespoke headboard designed by Jonathan with cushions in Cowtan & Tout's fabric.

Caldwell Winery TASTING ROOM

"Every room has to tell a story," says Rachman, recalling the elaborate narrative he crafted for the Caldwell Winery showhouse. It is an epic tale of cinematic proportions. Rachman envisioned the property's nineteenth-century cheese-making barn as the new residence of an English family who had traveled from the United Kingdom to Malacca, sailing east at the invitation of Sir Stamford Raffles, founder of the city of Singapore, where they would establish roots. Rachman imagined the family as generations of explorers and businessmen active in Batavia (present-day Jakarta), and Sumatra, who suddenly found themselves the heirs to a Napa vineyard. Physically realizing the storyline, Rachman created a space rich with English and Asian treasures, imagining the barn as "a straight-up English Colonial-era tasting room and the proprietor's private bath."

Juxtaposing old and new, Rachman preserved the rustic original elements of the barn, giving it a lavish layering of one-off pieces: an array of antique portraits (one of them is, in fact, of the Caldwell family); an old church pew found at an estate sale in nearby Atherton that he made plush with leather cushions secured by polished-nickel horse bits; Lucite spindle chairs; a zebra rug; and a modern st chair by Ralph Lauren. Rachman gave the existing wood counter a new marble top with a scalloped edge ("It's glorious!" he says) and stenciled the walls with a design he found on a match holder. "I wanted this room to function as a kitchen, as well as a communal tasting room where the winery could hold private parties and gatherings," he says. The bathroom, designed as "a masculine retreat after a day of supervising the winery," is focused on the materiality of the natural stone walls and the antique copper tub, an original feature. Throughout the rooms are fabrics from his collection for Ellis Dunn Textiles.

FACING PAGE
Ancestral portraits from England and the United States surround a Hudson lounge chair by Ralph Lauren. Among the paintings hangs a photograph of the current Mr. and Mrs. Caldwell, embellished with a 22-carat-gold pattern discovered on a pair of Javanese carved mirrors.

PAGES 104–5
The kitchen is a contemporary take on a traditional tasting room. The island is patinated with a natural teak color and Jonathan has added a thick slab of Carrara marble, butcher-block style.

RAFFLES HOTEL
LEMON CURD

RIGHT
Great Grandfather Caldwell rests amongst antiquarian tomes from the family library.

FACING PAGE
A stripped-oak vanity sits under a vintage French mirror in the master bathroom.

PAGES 108–9
Jonathan envisaged this patinated copper bathtub in a masculine retreat after a day supervising the winery.

D is

LEFT
Nickle horse bits on leather straps hold the bench seat-cushions in position.

FACING PAGE
Jonathan took his color cues from the natural verdigris stone walls. To cover the chair, he chose Belgian linen from Ellis Dunn.

PAGES 112–13
Billy the goat, a vintage display prop from the now defunct I. Magnin department store, greets visitors at the door of the tasting room.

HAVANA
Anna Karenina

A Collector's Library

SAN FRANCISCO DECORATOR SHOWCASE HOUSE

"I wanted to create a room with a classic European sensibility combined with a touch of the industrial," says Rachman of the moody, gentlemanly library he created as a showcase space. Inspired by his own passion for collecting, the room is home to a carefully selected group of objects. The tip of an American World War II A-26B bomber hangs over the fireplace, opposite a photograph of an Airbus 330 wing-tip taken by the designer on his iPhone mid-flight. The mantel displays a collection of primitive stone farming tools from his native Indonesia—souvenirs from his last trip to Bali—while the sculptures of *Loro Bionyo*—traditional figures of a wedding couple—are a further nod to his Javanese heritage. The preservation of such cultural artifacts is key to Jonathan's ethos and appreciation for global design. "Surround yourself with souvenirs of your life—things that reflect your travels and passions," he says. "A room should look collected and curated rather than staged or shopped." Here, it's a case of European chic melding naturally with Javanese exoticism. Traditional French fauteuils and antique, leather-bound books join mysterious jars of spices and maps of faraway lands for a truly worldly feel.

Vintage textiles, a Chinese abacus, and even an antique, ceramic hot-water bottle add a sense of nostalgia. As a backdrop for these collections, and to pull together the room's existing, mismatched woodwork, Rachman selected Benjamin Moore's Graphite in high gloss, a shade with associations of his time in Paris, echoed further by the gray marble fireplace surround. It's a room that tells a story, both real and imagined, through creative fantasy. Objects evoke curiosity and wonderment, thus inspiring conversation, and human connection. The library was a perfect opportunity for Rachman to express his signature approach to design: less formulaic, uncontrived, classic, and timeless, yet current and contemporary.

FACING PAGE
To unite mismatched woodwork, Jonathan applied four coats of Benjamin Moore's high-gloss paint in Graphite. The shade worked beautifully with the marble fire-surround and is a throwback to his time in Paris. The handsome cane-backed chair next to the fireplace was picked up at an estate sale in California.

PAGES 116–17
One of a kind: Above the fire surround hangs the wing tip of a World War II bomber. Jonathan removed the paintwork to expose the original aluminium patina. In a nod to sustainability, Jonathan has also repurposed and reused: the circular display table began life as a found industrial object, while the pendant lights were originally chicken feeders.

RIGHT
A perfect marriage of East and West. Vintage French apothecary jars meet antique Indonesian spice trays.

FACING PAGE
An industrial scaffolding rack displays further pieces from Jonathan's personal collection of ephemera, including French burlap linens, equestrian engravings, and a ceremonial headdress from the island of Sumba in Eastern Indonesia.

34
HW
Mackintosh's
Geneve

RESERVED FOR THE MASTER
ARMELLE BARON
CHRISTIAN SARRAMON
Allen & Hanburys

LEFT
A wooden Javanese tray holds some of Jonathan's most sentimental pieces. The *Loro Blonyo* sculptures in the background were picked up on a trip to Bali.

FACING PAGE
Jonathan is a keen collector of antique busts. This one not only anchors the room but sets the mood: "Oh, if this bust could talk," says Jonathan.

LEFT
A group of silhouettes, the oldest a sixteenth-century miniature, sits side by side with a Javanese batik stamp and a collection of andirons.

HOUSES OF PARIS

J. Rachman Studio and Showroom

"I had a crush on this building for years!" Rachman recalls of his San Francisco shop and studio. There was always a certain romance about the vacant storefront on Market Street, with its sky-high ceilings and picture windows. Built in 1911, La Salle, a former piano shop, was every bit as anachronistic as its façade would suggest. When Rachman finally stepped inside, having observed it for years, the ceilings were still lined with sheet music, the terrazzo mosaics intact, and the hardwood floors in good shape. The sense of drama was intoxicating to him. "It was like being in Paris! So, I took a breath, signed the longest lease of my life, and set about transforming the space." The bones were good, and Rachman's eponymous atelier now resembles a chic Parisian curiosity shop. His bold, calligraphic signature runs across the windows like a comet in gold leaf. Impossible to ignore and with a magnetic draw, it's difficult to pass by. The front of the 2,000-square-foot (185-m²) space is home to the "living room," a cozy enclave dominated by a bespoke red sofa. Trays of vintage glassware and hand-painted china sit amongst the designer's collection of favorite bibelots from around the world, including equestrian accoutrements like riding boots, saddles, and horsehair tassels. But the most striking feature in the tableau is the custom artwork behind the sofa. A friend gave Rachman a black-and-white photograph of a newlywed couple from Welahan, the Indonesian village from which Rachman's father hails. He enlarged and multiplied the image on a piece of Plexiglas to ghost-like effect, creating an unusual conversation piece. This is a deeply personal space (his design office is located at the rear of the building), but it's a place where all are welcome. "The greatest joy of the store is meeting people and exchanging stories," Rachman says. "I used to dream of opening a shop here. And now, here I am." Some things are just meant to be.

FACING PAGE
Design rediscovered: Jonathan wanted to give San Francisco the kind of store you'd discover on a quiet street in Paris, a shop full of curiosities where you can browse and touch things from centuries ago. The "living room" is home to everything from a Moroccan chandelier to a mid-century brass sofa. The Italian silk pillows are by Alexandra Foster.

PAGES 126–27
East meets West: Jonathan has brought together a collection of enticing patterns in a line of screen-printed linens for Ellis Dunn. Inspired by the women in his life, he christened the collection "Sisters," a tribute to the women who have helped and inspired him. "It's Left Bank meets Bali," he says.

421
424
425
NAPOLEON

FACING PAGE
Artisanal: Cushions held in position by Jonathan's bespoke nickel and leather straps.

ABOVE
Jonathan has a knack for pairing the unlikely. Seashells from small fishing villages in Southeast Asia sit happily with old-world curiosities from all corners of the globe.

PAGES 130–31
A blue coral branch sits amongst a sea of hand-painted glass and china, each piece personally selected by Jonathan.

FACING PAGE
A perfect marriage of the past and present: A heavily embroidered ceremonial livery is displayed next to pieces from Jonathan's own line of fine Italian leather goods.

LEFT
A pearlescent nautilus shell rests on a stack of Jonathan's vintage dinner wear. "It's all about the mix," he says.

FACING PAGE
Jonathan saved the store's original hardwood floors and stained them. The soaring ceilings allowed him to install a custom display-case to show off his bibelots in high style.

ABOVE
Austrian cut-crystal glassware and a Spode cup and saucer.

ABOVE
Occasionally, Jonathan finds photographs of strangers and becomes curious about their lives. "Some I've had so long they've begun to feel like family," he says.

FACING PAGE AND PAGES 138–39
The store is abundant with textures, from the mixed tones of the tiled floor to the patinated metalwork sconces. "I want people to come in, take a look around and be inspired—even if the only thing they take home with them is a good idea."

Luxury
SANDRA JORDAN
DEDAR
for people who don't drink. When
in the morning, that's as good
to feel all day."
FRANK SINATRA

GIN

THE ARM
MBLAY LES GONESSE
VENUE
BERGER
N.C.

Loro Blonyo Vignette

SAN FRANCISCO FALL ART AND ANTIQUES SHOW

Rachman's entry vignette for the antiques show was inspired, in part, by the sixtieth wedding anniversary of his parents, and designed around his *Loro Blonyo* wallpaper, which references the "Inseparable Couple," traditional Javanese figures that represent a pair of lovers, and are often given as wedding presents. But here, in his paper produced in collaboration with de Gournay, he has illustrated the relationship, somewhat cheekily, with monkeys. "As the show's theme was 'Animalia: Animal Imagery in Antiques and Art,' I turned my parents into Balinese monkeys from the Ubud Monkey Forest," explains Rachman. "Legend says that these primates were the descendants of the royal family. While my parents are not royal consorts of any sort, in my heart, they are the true royal lovers." The fanciful landscape in which the monkeys frolic is an hommage to his homeland and the lush greenery of his favorite island, Bali. Temples and traditional dwellings can be seen beyond the checkered umbrellas and through the palm trees, plants and orchids, as fishing boats sail along the river. It's an idyllic scene that is pure fantasy, yet it intrinsically reflects who Rachman is. "I insist on staying true to myself in what I do, and how I behave or dress or shop, as well as how I design," he says. "I can only be me." To furnish the space, Rachman paired a Javanese rattan settee and armchair set with an umbrella that echoes those seen in the wallpaper. Rounding out the space are contemporary metal and stone tables, a vintage landscape photo from the Peter Fetterman Gallery in Santa Monica, and fabrics from the designer's collection for Bolt Textiles. Exotic pink and red flowers featured in the vignette, too, of course. "No room is complete without flowers," says the designer. "I'm hopelessly romantic."

FACING PAGE
Loro Blonyo:
A detail of Jonathan's wallpaper for de Gournay. The fanciful hand-painted design was inspired by his parents' sixtieth wedding anniversary and the traditional Javanese wedding sculptures known as *Loro Blonyo*.

PAGES 142–43
Jonathan introduced texture to his vignette with a vintage rattan settee and armchair. A large, checkered umbrella echoes those seen in the wallpaper design, while metal and stone tables round out the space.

FACING PAGE
A blue coral sculpture from Eastern Indonesia is displayed in front of the exotic landscape in which the monkeys frolic.

ABOVE
A pair of Belgian linen Dharmi cushions from Jonathan's Sisters Collection for Ellis Dunn.

ABOVE
Jonathan created a simple arrangement of orchids and calla lilies to complete his tableau. He placed them on a bespoke brass bench topped with cowhide.

FACING PAGE
"Balinese legend has it that monkeys were the descendants of the royal family," explains Jonathan.

PAGES 148–49
A photograph of Jonathan's parents rests in front of a carved *Loro Blonyo* sculpture. "My parents really are the 'Inseparable Couple,'" he says.

An Art House

"There's nothing that breaks my heart more than a beautiful room that's unused," says Rachman, but that certainly isn't a worry for this bohemian Bay Area home imbued with a welcoming spirit. The historic house greets guests with an inviting, glassed-in porch; stepping inside reveals colorful interiors with myriad places that beckon visitors to relax and stay a while. In the living room, Rachman painted purple accent walls—one with the fireplace and one with the cocktail bar—a color that sets off the sandy-hued velvet sofa and armchairs. Two window nooks flood the room with natural light; in one, Rachman placed the owner's grand piano, in the other he placed a wing chair for reading or listening to music. The room, in fact the whole house, is filled with a collection of whimsical items—vintage French advertising posters, a carousel horse—that beg to tell their stories. In the formal dining room, mix-and-match chairs with different upholstery fabrics create a *laissez-faire* feel, and an antique curio cabinet was repurposed for stemware. Just off the kitchen (its geometric tile floors themselves a conversation starter), is an informal dining area presided over by an enchantingly outrageous vintage poster for a French suspender manufacturer. The library is a quieter retreat, where the designer paired such seemingly divergent items as a Mies van der Rohe chair with an Asian trunk—but it works. "The juxtaposition of the old and the new, of expected and unexpected moments, relaxes everything and makes a house feel unfussy," he explains. That free-spirited approach flows throughout the bedrooms, too, which reveal such temptations as a vintage rattan chaise in a bay window and an antique, iron day-bed enveloped with a playful monkey-patterned wallpaper. "Buy what you love, and you will always find a home for it," encourages Rachman.

FACING PAGE
In front of a Mies van der Rohe Barcelona chair are a silver wishbone sculpture, an antique cigar-mold, and a tiger-stone-studded curio box. The dusty-pink cushion is trimmed with antique gold-bullion braid.

PAGES 152–53
The kitchen and dining spaces are made visually distinct from each other through their contrasting floor patterns. While the dining room's wooden floors have a dark-grained patina, the kitchen is tiled in a brightly colored harlequin pattern in terracotta.

THOS HORROCKS ~ BOOT & SHOE MKR
AT THE SIGN OF THE GOLDEN LEG
17 55
No LONDON WALL

ABOVE
The timeless silhouette of a wingback chair, updated with a bold striped velvet. The carousel horse is vintage and the rug is Persian.

FACING PAGE
Monkeys run riot in a guestroom. The Procuratie facades of St. Mark's Square in Venice provide a primates' playground for mischievous monkeys in Cole & Son's Procuratie Con Vista wallpaper.

The iron daybed is antique and covered in a bespoke S. Harris coverlet and Pierre Frey skirt. Jonathan lavished the windows with tailored pelmets and roman blinds in Pindler linen with contrast bands by Pierre Frey.

PAGES 156–57
The organic nature of the natural wood floor adds a warm, inviting feel to the master bedroom. The cane-backed campaign bed is overlooked by a Sabine reading lamp from Arteriors.

CHANEL
CHANEL
CHANEL

V. Marcadé - ART D'UKRAINE
FUTURISM
EL LISSITZKY
THEATRE IN REVOLUTION
MALEVICH Great Modern Masters CAMEO/ABRAMS
Hayden
L'AGE D'HOMM

St. Regis
SAN FRANCISCO

"There's a fine line between collection and clutter—don't allow objects to overwhelm," advises Rachman. "Know when less is more, and when more truly is more." In the case of an art-filled residence at the St. Regis Hotel in San Francisco, a warm but minimalist interior was the goal. Starting with a palette of creamy whites, dove grays, and ocean blues, Rachman layered the spaces with geometric pieces and textural fabrics. In the living room, an extra-long, linen-upholstered sofa runs the length of the room, joined by a square, stone-topped coffee table and two organically shaped ottomans. A pair of angular, wood-frame chairs, upholstered with a striated pattern of blues and grays, are designed to do double duty in the home. They provide additional seating for the living room or, if swiveled, become part of the adjacent office area. There, the designer continued the palette but shifted to smooth metal finishes for a streamlined, industrial feel. A wall-mounted console keeps the space from feeling heavy. Shelves are neatly lined with storage boxes, small artworks, and books that reflect the home owner's collecting interests: Manuel Neri, Jeanloup Sieff, Jock Sturges, Peter Lindbergh. The main living area is also open to the kitchen and dining areas, where Rachman paired sleigh-back chairs with a Saarinen-style table. Adding warmth and patina is a selection of antiques—a giltwood console, a drop-front secretary desk, a painted and gilded klismos chair—thoughtfully placed throughout the home. In the bedroom, a deep-green leather headboard and abstract painting, one of several in the home, are illuminated by a brass lamp. A marble-clad bathroom offers a distinctly spa-like retreat. "I always know from the beginning when a project will turn out amazingly," says the designer. "When clients fully trust me, I know my hands are not tied and that's when my creative freedom thrives."

FACING PAGE
Clear thinking: Paired down and stripped back, a monochrome canvas by Nathan Oliveira coexists harmoniously with a carved French dining chair and Dutch drop-front secretary desk.

PAGES 160–61
Sculpturally stunning: A torso by Manuel Neri stands behind a bespoke Metrocubo sectional sofa by Living Divani. The armchair is by Jean Royère and the coffee table is made of brass and shagreen.

Manuel Ne
ICONS OF THE
PETER LIN

HERB RITTS
NTURY
JEANLOUP SIEFF
ERGH
Jock Sturges New Work 1996–2000

FACING PAGE
Shapes play a key role in the restrained look of the room, from the organically shaped ottomans by Patricia Urquiola to Boris Deutsch's geometric *Dancers*, framed on the wall.

ABOVE
Textural beauty: inlaid shagreen on the surface of the coffee table.

PAGES 164–65
Continuing the pared-back theme, a Saarinen-style dining table is surrounded by a collection of carved French chairs. A mixed-media collage by Hahn provides the only decorative relief.

余市

FACING PAGE
Seen through the doorway, on the far wall, *Deux Femmes* by Le Corbusier.

LEFT
At ease: A neoclassical klismos chair, carved, painted, and gilded.

PAGES 168–69
A bespoke leather bedhead is the focal point in this carefully balanced scheme. A still life by Polish cubist Henri Hayden hangs to the left. For pillows, Jonathan chose Priati from his own Sisters Collection with Ellis Dunn.

Bold & Beautiful

Simplicity and elegance—and a few ladylike touches—are the hallmarks of this new Bay Area condo. Faux marble walls in the entryway create an immediate sense that this space is something different. Stepping further inside confirms it. Despite its small scale, Rachman made the rooms feel generous by repeating patterns and materials, and by carefully choosing moments for bold color. In the living room, a petit sofa and side chair are joined by an ottoman upholstered in the same geometric print selected for the throw pillows, creating a feeling of balance and movement. To save space, the designer mounted the television on the wall above a lacquered console that provides extra storage and room for stools tucked underneath. "Edit, edit, and edit," says Rachman. "I don't believe in trends; I believe in longevity." And throughout he has chosen clean-lined pieces that can grow and adapt with the homeowner. In the open kitchen and dining room, Rachman cleverly repeated the same black-and-gold seating design for the barstools and the dining chairs, again creating rhythm in the space. Artful additions include rose quartz pendant lights above the counter and Randal Ford's striking photograph of a black swan. The designer took each of the bedrooms in a different direction. One is ethereal, with a palette of soft celadon and cream, grounded with dark, cerused-oak nightstands. The other is a brighter palette, with emerald-green velvet chosen for the curtains and headboard, all set off by the bed wall's dramatic black wallpaper with thin bands of gold veining. "Texture, color, and scale. They are my holy trinity," he adds.

FACING PAGE
Black Swan No. 1 by Randal Ford hangs dramatically above a glossy Peso table by Holly Hunt. The steel and leather Bardot chairs are by Gabriel Scott.

ABOVE
Rose-quartz pendant lights by Gabriel Scott are suspended above a bespoke kitchen island with concealed cabinetry. The units blend seamlessly into the background.

FACING PAGE
Textural triumph: A free-standing Horn floor lamp made of crushed silk and metal rests against Zinc Textile's Marbleous wall covering. Opposite is *Rejang Dancer* by Balinese artist Tjandra Hutama.

FACE PAGE
A bespoke bed frame is the focal point in this beautifully balanced scheme. A pair of antique intaglios hang above a contemporary white porcelain lamp.

ABOVE
The living room features Caste's Malta sofa covered in Great Plains' Royal Alpaca fabric. Jonathan chose Palazzo Velatura fabric to cover the bespoke ottoman and cushions.

oscar

FACING PAGE
The guest bedroom walls provide an unexpected shimmer of light and are lined with Gregorius/Pineo's Glint wall covering in Night Roof. An Amelia Regency nightstand in brass and shagreen sits next to a bespoke scalloped headboard covered in Scalamandre Nabab Myrtle velvet by Shears & Window.

ABOVE
A brass floor lamp stands beside a small Italian club chair by Coup Studios.

A'musing in Paris

SAN FRANCISCO DECORATOR SHOWCASE HOUSE

Is there a more glamorous duo than Hubert de Givenchy and Audrey Hepburn? Their friendship—and particularly the iconic Jacques Scandelari photograph of the couple walking along the Seine—was the inspiration behind Rachman's cheerfully spring-green showhouse living room. "I imagine them returning to Givenchy's *salon vert* on Rue de Grenelle to enjoy the afternoon while 'April in Paris' plays softly in the background," says the designer. "My first impression of the room was its grandeur, with its massive marble fireplace oozing charm and time-worn patina. The traditional feel of the room was stately; with its high ceiling, however, it felt dated and heavy." Knowing he wanted to revive the space with a "fresh, chic, and airy feel," Rachman immediately called his friends at de Gournay. "I wanted to create a custom wallpaper that would give the room distinction, fantasy, and delight," he explains. To instill the room with the energy of springtime, Rachman and de Gournay designed a custom silk wallpaper with a hand-painted, hand-embroidered, "silk tree" pattern. Its palette of green, lavender, silver, and chartreuse was, in part, inspired by a Royal Doulton "Countess"-pattern plate Rachman found in Italy. The room is anchored by a tufted velvet sofa and a pair of 1920s wing chairs, above which floats an intricate plastered ceiling, its decorative rosettes picked out in 24-carat gold by artist Caroline Lizarraga. Lambrequin pelmets at the windows and a brass chandelier inspired by the church bells of San Miguel de Allende heighten the room's drama. With its multiple seating areas, including the wall-to-wall banquette bedecked with lavish fringe, it's a room that Rachman hoped would inspire conversation and time enjoyed with friends and family. As Hepburn so famously said, "The best thing to hold onto in life is each other."

FACING PAGE
Patina: Jonathan loved the original fireplace and built his design around it. To accentuate the ceiling's plasterwork he commissioned Caroline Lizarraga to individually gild each rosette with 24-carat gold-leaf flakes. The San Miguel chandelier by Boyd consists of some one thousand solid brass tear drops.

PAGES 180–81
The angular wingback chairs and tufted sofa are covered in varying shades of emerald and kelly-green velvet from Lee Jofa and Designers Guild. A scallop-edged lambrequin pelmet frames the south-facing window.

RIGHT
Details: Silk Tree, a bespoke design by de Gournay, features hand-painted, hand-embroidered blossoming silk tree branches set against an emerald, dyed-silk background. Jonathan picked out the unique shade of green from a vintage Royal Doulton plate.

FACING PAGE
A sculpted resin console by Ironies strikes a modern note paired with a French gilt mirror.

PRIVATE HOUSES OF
Living with History
OLIVER MESSEL
In the Theatre of Design
CHRISTIAN

FACING PAGE
A pair of ebony-framed gilt medallions depicting spring and summer hang above a bespoke banquette. The decorative silk pillows in shades of green and white are from Alexandra Foster.

LEFT
Tream Pickings: Houlès beaded fringe trims the base of Jonathan's bespoke banquette.

RIGHT
A'Musing in Paris by Marc-Antoine Coulon.

FACING PAGE
Florals and foliage: Jonathan chose and arranged the flowers personally. His goal was to intoxicate visitors with the fragrance of Cherry blossoms, rosemary and lilac's.

PAGES 188–89
One of the most important pieces in the room is Jacques Scandelari's photograph of couturier Hubert de Givenchy and his muse, Audrey Hepburn. It was Jonathan's inspiration for the room. He hung the print over a Louis XVI commode as an hommage to a pair of the most iconic talents in the world of fashion.

ASSOULINE
IVILEGED LIFE

A Victorian Renaissance

"There had to be a sense of equilibrium between the old and the new," says Rachman. "Nobody wants to live in a big old Victorian house that looks like Grandma's attic." Nineteenth-century Victorian townhouses are quintessentially San Francisco. The architecture is familiar and nostalgic, lining many of the city's most sought-after and iconic neighborhoods. When Rachman was invited to refresh a fine example in the Pacific Heights neighborhood, he jumped at the chance. "I had already designed this home for the previous owners, a young family with a baby, and the chance to do it all over again for new clients was an opportunity I just couldn't pass up," he says. Rachman knew the building inside out, but he was surprised by just how much he had in common with its new inhabitants. When they saw the house, it hit all the right notes. Rachman's previous refurbishment had struck a chord with them because his design was thoughtful and sympathetic to the home's many original architectural details. The day they bought the house, they called him. They knew they wanted to honor the home's age with decorative wallpapers and antiques, but they also knew they didn't want it to feel oppressive or stuffy. Rachman worked to temper the home's formality with contemporary touches. "Paint brown furniture to revive it, reupholster old pieces, and gild as much as possible," he says playfully. The designer also strove to give each space a surprise, from unique light fixtures ("A lavish decorative fixture is like your Taffin brooch," he says) and modern art to textiles and curiosities picked up on his travels. "It's the marriage of the old and the new that I love. I think it's a marriage that's going to last."

FACING PAGE
In the living room Jonathan paired a Coup d'État sofa with a contemporary coffee table by Kravet. A silvery rug by Stark echoes the walls painted in Benjamin Moore's Gray Owl. For a whimsical twist, Jonathan added a vintage Argentinian shell sculpture.

FACING PAGE
The silk Askew wallpaper is by de Gournay and the Lucite chandelier is vintage and was picked up by Jonathan in London. Its style mirrors the original art deco sconces in Claridge's ballroom.

LEFT
The kitchen preparation area is made to measure, allowing enough space to prepare a large dinner. The copper island and faucets are by Waterworks and the copper hood was handcrafted in Denmark for Abbaka.

influential styl
DECO PARISIAN

LEFT
The family room features a sofa, ottoman, and chair by Jean-Louis Deniot for Baker, while Jonathan chose Hermès's Equateur and Fortuny's Vivaldi fabrics for the throw pillows. The green ceramic gueridons are from J. Rachman Design and deliver an unexpected pop of color to an otherwise neutral space, while providing a nod to the formal garden visible through the floor-to-ceiling glass doors.

LEFT
Outdoor elegance: The garden terrace features a suite of furniture. For the throw pillows, Jonathan chose fabrics from his Sisters Collection for Ellis Dunn and Duralee's Sedgewich fabric.

FACING PAGE
The grand double doors are painted in Benjamin Moore's Van Deusen Blue and open to reveal a traditional Victorian staircase. A sleek Portobello lantern by Vaughan hangs in the doorway.

LEFT
Flights of fancy: Fluted sconces display the homeowner's blue parrot candelabras on an upstairs landing.

FACING PAGE
Jonathan turned to Lee Jofa to dress the master bed in soft gray velvet. The mirrored side tables are by Ironies.

LEFT
In the bathroom a pair of Melissa Quartz sconces sit either side of symmetrically placed George I gilt mirrors. For the cushion on the Italian bench, Jonathan chose Fortuny's Melagrana fabric in aubergine and silver.

RIGHT
The chicest of dressing rooms is achieved with a restrained palette of gray and white. The walls are wrapped in Schumacher's Chinois Palais wallpaper, while the deep bay window is dressed in Designers Guild's Brera Striscia fabric. The passementerie was custom made by Décor de Paris and the Louis XVI linen-covered armchair is backed in Cowtan & Tout Fabric.

FACING PAGE
Above the Antoinette daybed by Kathy Kuo hangs a pencil drawing by Bonnie Beauchamp-Cooke. The Waldorf chandelier by Arteriors adds a contemporary touch to the room.

VREELAND MEMOS

A Modern Cottage

"This house used to be a simple cottage but then it was literally lifted up to accommodate a subterranean garage—but its historic façade was preserved," recalls Rachman of the San Francisco home he designed for long-time clients, a blended family of five. "They're big supporters of human rights and equality, truly a loving family," says Rachman, who even designed the couple's wedding. "The home is a modern cottage, very casual yet chic, but for me, no matter what the project, it always comes down to the human factor, and to making a home truly a nest," he continues. "The couple are art lovers with a growing collection—Picasso, Chagall, as well as contemporary artists—so we had to take that into consideration, too." Key to the design was creating a new master bedroom and defined spaces for each child, even if they had already fledged. The second aspect was comfort and practicality. "While casual in their lifestyle, they love to entertain, so we needed a large dining table and comfy, loungy sofas." To that end, Rachman placed four chairs and two long benches around the table and sourced a plush L-shaped sofa and sumptuous chairs and upholstered ottomans for the living room. The designer also put special emphasis on finding lighting designs that read more like sculpture, creating a tree-house room, and designing a wine cellar—another growing interest for the couple. "Accomplishing what they needed in a way that works in this 'stacked'-style modern cottage challenged my creativity in a positive and fun manner," Rachman reflects. "It was like solving a giant puzzle! Very rewarding."

FACING PAGE
On the wall, a pair of lithographs by Marc Chagall. The gallery wall continues to the left with a canvas by Eduardo Arranz-Bravo.

LEFT
Cloud chandelier by Apparatus sits above The Water's Rising dining table by Tod Von Mertens. Arden Home chairs and a pair of Giac settees by DLV from Coup d'État surround the table and provide the clients with a perfect view of their Picasso. At the opposite end of the room a more informal tone is set with a bespoke sectional sofa.

ABOVE
The Medusa Bloom chandelier by Ochre hangs over a custom island by Cardea Building.

FACING PAGE
In the family room, a canvas by Eduardo Arranz-Bravo hangs above a bespoke sectional sofa. The stool is by Arden Home.

RIGHT
A custom bed by Arden Home sits in front of a pair of ottomans covered in fabric from Pierre Frey. Above the bed hangs a photograph of surfer Kelly Slater taken by Aaron Chang. To the left of the bed is a chair by Palecek.

JOHN LE CARRE
1776 DAVID McCULLOUGH
Gotthard Schuh
The New Formal INTERIORS BY JAMES AMAN
The Fisher Collection
ANNIE LEIBOVITZ A Photographer's Life 1990–2005

St. Helena

A WINE COUNTRY ESTATE

"Warm, cozy, elegant" was the brief for a contemporary family home in Napa Valley, Northern California's premier wine region. "The clients wanted something different," Rachman explains. "They didn't want to live in just another one of those 'identikit' country houses, but a spectacular home with quiet luxury, where they can entertain." It also needed to merge indoor and outdoor living to take full advantage of the extraordinary scenery. (The property includes some twenty acres [eight hectares], fourteen [five and a half] of which are planted with a private Cabernet Sauvignon vineyard.) "I wanted to add a touch of romance to an otherwise strictly sleek design," Rachman continues. He took his cues directly from the surrounding landscape of wooded hillsides and tidy rows of deciduous vines that come right up to the house. He kept the palette neutral, occasionally pulling in moments of color, like the sunny yellow chair in the family room and the persimmon-hued chair in the office. "I wanted to blend my love of European classics with the modern foundation of the property," he continues, "but the challenge was creating harmony without appearing contrived." Sourcing pieces locally, as well as from Italy, Germany, France, and Indonesia, Rachman crafted rooms that are at once subtle and striking. Countering the hard lines of the stone and glass foyer and adjacent wine cellar is an unexpected series of large-scale neoclassical landscape paintings. An elaborate rococo mirror and monumental crystal chandelier create a dialogue with the minimalist dining table and chairs, while a pair of Italian cerule-style chairs feel right at home with more contemporary pieces in the living room. Rachman kept the bedrooms simple and serene, with spa-like bathrooms. He gave the guest house a similar stylistic treatment but brought in a deeper palette with greens, reds, and purples, all inspired by the landscape as it changes through the seasons.

FACING PAGE
The estate's extensive surroundings feature an abundance of outdoor venues, including the pool, complete with spa.

PAGES 214–15
The crosscut travertine walls make a strong architectural impact and flood the dining room with light. The room's lofty proportions are heightened further by the vast Louis XV chandelier, hung above the Seamless dining table. Around the table there's an eclectic collection of contemporary leather chairs and vintage linen-covered wingback chairs.

KABINETT & KAMMER
The Lives of Others Simon Watson

PAGES 216–17
The refined and the raw, the classical and the modern, all merge easily behind the vast glass doors of the living room. Pieces of varying styles and periods all happily coexist: a sculpture by Stephen de Staebler sits comfortably with an Aland wingback chair by Jean de Merry. A mid-century lamp works well with a pair of Italian campaign chairs, while the whole room is anchored by the cheerily patterned Stark rug.

FACING PAGE
On the wall is a vintage mirror from J. Rachman. The Welles chandelier is by Gabriel Scott.

ABOVE
In the family room a yellow Buffa chair from Coup d'État adds a pop of color. The pillows are from Firmamenta.

FACING PAGE
In the kitchen and dining area the palette is clean and contemporary. Continuing the pared-back theme, Jonathan selected a Donghia Raleigh table in satin-finished walnut, and a set of leather-backed Isabel chairs by Flexform.

ABOVE
The kitchen cupboards are concealed behind bespoke zebrawood cabinetry. An Agnes chandelier in brushed brass is suspended over the bespoke high-gloss kitchen island.

FACING PAGE
Suspended cable racking provides a dramatic way to store an extensive collection of fine wines, which appear to float in front of a window.

ABOVE
The structure and exterior architecture are in a predominantly neutral gray tone, punctuated with organic materials.

RIGHT
The master bedroom is calm and paired back. The fitted bed is bespoke, the table lamps and bench by Holly Hunt. The only touch of drama is the oversized Halo chandelier.

MAN IN THE MIDDLE

Park Views

This two-story penthouse sits atop one of San Francisco's most celebrated architectural landmarks, and its views of an historic park make it an all the more extraordinary location. But inside, time hadn't been kind. "We were stunned by the datedness of the place," Rachman recalls of his first visit. "Every inch had been upholstered with silk, but it had become run down. The house felt stuffy and dated, not to mention dusty!" To kickstart the renovation, Rachman devised a design scheme that would make the interiors "current, but long-lasting," he says. "No matter when you visit a house I've designed, it stays undated," he adds. "I think it's a mistake to be trendy or to follow a certain design hipness." Here, the designer opted for a bold palette that leaps quickly but logically from black-gloss reception rooms to a gleaming green kitchen to a blue-lacquered den. Gone is the musty silk, and in is the sparkle. Original details like the plaster ceilings were enhanced with gilding, and traditional motifs (Greek key patterns, fretwork, chinoiserie, toile) all do their part to ramp up the home's stately style. "I drew inspiration from the clients' lifestyle, as well as my own travels," says Rachman. "Guests may visit this penthouse and feel they're in London's Berkeley Square neighborhood, or the Marais in Paris, or on Fifth Avenue in Manhattan. I wanted this penthouse to feel cosmopolitan." As with all of Rachman's projects, here antiques sit comfortably with contemporary art and design pieces, and surprises abound—from a peppy orange banquette to a gold-hued powder room. "I love clients who aren't afraid of bold colors, or of antique and modern pieces juxtaposed with each other. Patina and pristine can commingle," he says, adding fearlessly: "If you're going to max out on style, then really max out!"

FACING PAGE
Glittering reflections in the dusty-rose en suite parlor as the French chandelier shimmers in the afternoon sunlight. The neutral tones of the wall color are punctuated by pops of pink in the Louis XVI-style bergère and bullion-trimmed ottoman.

FACING PAGE
An Italian fruitwood armchair has been refreshed with new leather upholstery and Old Weavers' Taos velvet in the home office. For the bespoke ottoman Jonathan chose Thibaut velvet from Anna French. The area rug is by Stark.

RIGHT
To the left of the balustrade stands a marble plinth displaying a plaster bust picked up in Spain. The staircase is outfitted in Stark's Beaton Black carpet.

RIGHT
Cocktails: A mid-century Jetson lamp is displayed on a brass bar cart by William Sonoma.

FACING PAGE
Dark deco: The high-gloss sheen of the polished walls extends to the hardwood floors, lacquered a rich, dark ebony. An Adele waterfall chandelier hangs above a bespoke gilded dining table surrounded by a collection of Chintaly rollback chairs. A group of French and Vietnamese candle holders act as a centerpiece.

PAGES 232–33
Dramatic flourishes reach even the kitchen. The cabinets are painted in Benjamin Moore's zesty Emerald Isle. To cover the Abacus stools, Jonathan chose Kravet's Acid Palm fabric. The bespoke mosaic backsplash is by Waterworks.

Decorating with Flowers

RIGHT
In the master bedroom a pencil drawing by Picasso hangs above a Louis XVI-style caned chaise. The windows are dressed in Stroheim's Kasseri floral silk and Jonathan discovered the Jansen-inspired nightstand at Chairish. A low bench is the perfect bed companion and increases the sense of luxury in the room.

FACING PAGE
De Gournay's delicately patterned Gold Bullion Rateau paper weaves a beautiful layer of decorative interest in the bathroom.

TULUM
BIBLIO-STYLE
MCALPINE POETRY OF PLACE

Ashbury Heights

"I refuse to do a project where I am not having fun," say Rachman, only half-joking. "And this project is one of the most fun experiences I've ever had as a designer." The home, a grand Edwardian villa built in 1908, doesn't disappoint on any aspect of its design—new or original. "I believe in honoring a house's origins and history, as well as its style and energy, and I wanted to preserve as much of the interior architecture here as possible, especially the colorful stained-glass windows and antique, embossed wallcoverings. But I also needed to bring the house into 2022 by updating some of the finishes." After Rachman presented his design concept, the owners essentially gave him carte blanche, not only in decorating the interiors but also in rearranging the spaces. With their blessing, the designer turned a family room into an onyx-clad wine cellar; transformed the breakfast room into a wine lounge; expanded the master suite, which affords incredible ocean views; and renovated every bedroom and bathroom. The open-plan kitchen and informal family spaces were also revived, as were the front and back gardens. "Everything is custom, from the de Gournay wall coverings to the banquettes and window seats," adds Rachman. (Even the nursery was given a luxurious pink wallpaper decorated with butterflies—and a chic Lucite crib.) "This house is a perfect example of my philosophy, 'More is never enough,' where patterns collide and colors are juxtaposed in a way that might frighten some, yet the entire house is cohesive—and stunning! These clients are people who appreciate the finer things in life—wine, champagne, dining, fashion, and travel—and we connected on such a level that if felt as if we'd known each other for decades. This project is a dream come true."

FACING PAGE
In the sitting area of the master bedroom Jonathan paired a tufted Century ottoman with a pair of bespoke, leaf-green armchairs in Queen Victoria velvet. A ceramic gueridon echoes the forest-green palette of the room. On the wall is a sculpture by Jesùs Pedraglio.

LEFT
In the living room Jonathan paired a traditional tufted sofa with a mid-century Silas Seandel coffee table. To give the original carved fire surround some extra sparkle he accented the details with traditional water-gilding. To the right of the fireplace Jonathan installed a panel of de Gournay's St Laurent embroidered wallpaper.

RIGHT
De Gournay's golden wallpaper, Summer Night Blossom, sets the tone in the entrance hall.

FACING PAGE
In the dining room Koket's Ribbon table is surrounded by a set of Louis Philippe chairs Jonathan discovered at Thenadey in Paris. He re-covered them in a rich black velvet from Schumacher.

ERIC
METROPOLITAN LUXURY

FACING PAGE
Schumacher's classic Haruki Sisal in indigo offers a textural backdrop to this rather masculine seating area. Jonathan re-covered a vintage swivel chair in his signature Brothers fabric. For the bespoke tufted ottoman, he chose British Tan leather by Ellis Dunn.

LEFT
On the wall, a collection of reverse-glass nautical scenes flanks a Regency gilt convex mirror.

RIGHT AND FACING PAGE
In the kitchen Jonathan has covered French club chairs and mid-century ice cream stools in burgundy leather. For the curtains he chose velvet by Holland & Sherry.

The Vyrodas

RIGHT
A matching pair of 1940s Gustavian Louis XV-style chests sit either side of a carved and upholstered bedhead. The pineapple lamps are Italian parcel-gilt. For the pillows Jonathan chose Little Thistle fabric by Timorous Beasties. A French chaise has been re-covered in Brunschwig & Fils velvet with gimp by Décor de Paris.

RIGHT
Blooms and botanicals: a set of antiquarian botanical plates are displayed above a marble-topped commode by Baker. The elaborate, full-skirted curtains add a touch of softness to the scheme.

FACING PAGE
In the bathroom, clean lines create an uncluttered and elegant space. Jonathan chose a simple Voltaire scroll-topped bath from Waterworks. The bespoke window screen allows light to filter softly into the room, casting shadows on the mosaic marble floor tiles.

FACING PAGE
A marble bathroom is brightened by a vintage quatrefoil chandelier. The walls are covered in Manuel Canovas' Bengale Paprika wallpaper, with curtains and pelmet to match.

LEFT
A Louis Phillippe mirror hangs above a custom-painted vanity with hardware by Modern Matter. The Camilla alabaster sconces are trimmed with Zoffany's Arabella Barbetta bobbles.

FACING PAGE AND ABOVE In the pink: De Gournay's silk wallpaper, Butterflies, gives the nursery a light dreaminess. Originally planned as a guest room, the bespoke bed was replaced with a dusty-rose bassinet and a Cloud crib when the homeowner's situation changed. For the curtains and ottoman, Jonathan chose Designers Guild's Jardin des Plantes fabric.

RIGHT
A corner seating area furnished with a blue triangle lamp and a carved red lacquered chair. For the cushion, Jonathan chose blue and white Chinese Fret by Jim Thompson.

FACING PAGE
Palms and pagodas: The tented guest room is papered in Thibaut's South Sea wallpaper.

LEFT
A bordered lambrequin pelmet frames the small cusped window. A lipstick-red Chandy chandelier adds a pop of color to the room. Jonathan accessorized with English Ironstone plates in orange and blue.

Afterword

HANNAH CECIL GURNEY

I first met Jonathan almost a decade ago. We were brought together by the wonderful San Francisco Antique Show. Jonathan had been invited to design a vignette and de Gournay to create a bespoke wallcovering for that vignette. We were thrown into working together on a beautifully creative wallcovering inspired by Jonathan's native Indonesia. I was immediately struck by his exceptional energy, positivity, and humor. I assumed it must be something he turned on and off. No. It's always on.

Jonathan is an addiction and once you have spent time with him you want more. His zest for living is infectious. He has you on-the-floor with laughter... while at the same time he is compassionate, ridiculously generous (to a point that is irritating), and loving. He treats everyone like family. This, of course, extends to his clients. This means that the care and attention he takes with every project—from overall concept down to the detail of an arrangement of books on a shelf—is second to none.

Jonathan cares deeply about the way his clients will experience his interiors. He loves color and his rooms sing. His interiors instill a positive energy in those who enter them and you don't want to leave. His interiors are comfortable yet always luxurious, and never without a touch of drama.

Jonathan has incorporated our wallcoverings into many of his projects, but the one that has always been my favorite was his custom color of our "Silk Tree" design for his Givenchy-inspired Green Room at the San Francisco Decorator Showhouse. It was emeralds on emeralds on emeralds. The use of color in the room was spectacular; I never wanted to leave. It was so bold, but it didn't feel at all overwhelming. In fact, it felt refreshing and energizing, rich and bold with a dash of his signature, old-school style.

It's been a privilege to have watched Jonathan develop as an accomplished and internationally recognized designer. I see his spirit in each and every page of this book, which celebrates his lifelong passion for design. I hope you have enjoyed it as much as I have.

FACING PAGE
Hannah Cecil Gurney photographed in Jonathan's "A'Musing In Paris" show house, San Francisco, 2017.

Acknowledgments

JONATHAN RACHMAN

This book is dedicated to the craftsmen and women of Indonesia, and the classic architects and designers of the western world who unknowingly inspired me all my life.

It is dedicated to my parents, our Loro Blonyo—the inseparable couple—who not only exposed, showed and submerged me in beauty all my life, but allowed and encouraged me to pursue my passion from a very young age. They did not only teach me the word LOVE and compassion, but showered me with love, showed me what compassion means throughout my life. I also attribute to them my travel addiction, which was my design education: besides observing and learning from them, I was their permanent carry on!

I also want to dedicate this book to the women in my life: my sisters, Edna and Wewe; my grandmas, my aunts, Betty, Oen, and Li; and cousins, Tian, Siong, Peck, and Lely, who have contributed to my life experience and added to my knowledge in beauty. This also includes the women and men of our estate, who have lovingly dedicated their lives not only in keeping our home immaculate, but also in raising me as a child. To my kind teachers: Suster Dionis in the Netherlands; Ibu Kristen, Pak Tris, Ibu Susilowati, Ibu Kelas Tiga, and Ibu Theresia in Indonesia; Ms. Murphy, Ms. Nakashima, and Professor Bright in the United States, and M. Lasala in Switzerland: I am grateful for your support, guidance, and love.

I would not be here without the constant support and tremendous love from my amazingly patient and loving husband, Stephen: I love you today more than yesterday but less than tomorrow. Thank YOU for allowing me to be me in my professional and personal life. YOU were the first to encourage me to open my business; you have always been there since day one. My success is because of YOU. This book is our book. Eternity is too short, eternity is not long enough, my love.

ABOVE
Jonathan Rachman sketched by Marc-Antoine Coulon at Le Bristol, Paris, 2020.

Bob! I don't deserve to have you in my life, but you are. Your unconditional support, trust, and love to both Stephen and me are the very reason why we say you are our angel on earth.

Judith, mi hermana, JRD and I would not be here without you—I am indebted to you for your unwavering support, hard work, dedication and loyalty

To my JRD Ohana, mi sobrina Monica, Maria Luisa, Erik, Jeffrey, Yuni, your loyalty and dedication to JRD and me are more than I deserve.

To everyone who has contributed to JRD's inception and longevity, including our purveyors, workroom, and craftsmen worldwide, know that I have nothing but gratitude and respect for you.

To all the editors globally who not only have believed in my work and me, but who, as a group of professionals, have been responsible for putting my work and name out there for others to see and seek—I am also indebted to you. While I can't possibly mention everyone, allow me to mention: Paige, your ability to understand not only my work but also my true emotions is unparalleled; Mary-Jo, your kindness is as amazing as your talents. Kerryn, I am grateful to you and for your generosity. DDS, I cannot thank you enough for recognizing and championing my work. Doretta, your humility, kindness, compassion and love are truly inspiring, I am blessed to call you, my friend. Drea, I would not be here without you, and you are and will always be in my heart.

To my loyal clients, and to those who have believed in me from my early days as well as given me a chance: I am humbled by your trust and loyalty.

I am especially thankful to Marc Jacobs, Lisa Erspamer, Oprah Winfrey, Sarah Jessica Parker, and Madonna for giving me my start in the floral and design industry as well as the Four Seasons of San Francisco. It has been my honor for twenty years to serve and design for you. I am only as good as a designer as your trust in commissioning me—thank YOU!

A special appreciation to Mary Beth and David Shimmons for allowing me to put your house on the cover!

To my gorgeous wifey, Hannah, and her husband, Eddie, my private John Snow; to my English sister, Rachel, and my Superman, Jake; to my sister, the sweet, talented and beauty-full Jemma—and to Daddy Claud of de Gournay: thank YOU for not only supporting me, believing in me, and for including me in your journey, but also for making it so much fun to be in this industry! I shall never forget your generosity. More importantly, I am touched that you make me feel I have another family who truly understands my sense of design and the joy of living!

My dear Denise: I am touched, humbled and grateful for your generosity, friendship, loyalty, support and love! I can't imagine a world without you. In the sea of fake diamonds, you are the real deal: honest, authentic, and the biggest gem in the sea of cubic zirconia.

To the talented photographers: Jose Manuel Alorda, Douglas Friedman, Suzanna Scott, Aubrie Pick, Mark Leet, Drew Altizer, and every photographer whose work is showcased in this book: I am beyond grateful to all of you!

Marc-Antoine Coulon: thank you for the beautyfull illustrations and for my portrait; your talents are mesmerizing.

Finally: this book would never have materialized without the talents and passion of my co-author "Lady" Dean Rhys-Morgan who introduced me to Suzanne Tise-Isoré of Flammarion: I am truly touched by the both of you for your guidance and confidence in me—for that I am truly honored!

RIGHT
Jonathan at his Market Street studio surrounded by mementos. The orange glass pendant lights are from the movie *Anchorman*. The paintings are by Balinese students supported by Jonathan and his husband, Stephen. As Jonathan says, "Surround yourself with the things you love, and you will always find room for them."

LEO FUC

FRONT COVER
The chicest of living rooms in a Russian Hill home: René Bouché's 1959 portrait of model China Machado hangs on a custom shocking-pink colorway of de Gournay's Salon Vert chinoiserie wallpaper. The chaise was picked up at Chairish and lacquered a rich ebony.

EXECUTIVE DIRECTOR
Suzanne Tise-Isoré
Style & Design Collection

EDITORIAL COORDINATION
Lara Lo Calzo

GRAPHIC DESIGN
Lucrezia Russo

COPY EDITING
Lindsay Porter

PROOFREADING
Barbara Mellor

PRODUCTION
Corinne Trovarelli

COLOR SEPARATION
Atelier Frédéric Claudel, Paris

PRINTING
Indice, Barcelona, Spain

Flammarion S.A.
82, rue Saint Lazare
75009 Paris
editions.flammarion.com
@styleanddesignflammarion

22 23 24 3 2 1
ISBN: 978-2-08-024226-6
Legal Deposit: 09/2022

PHOTOGRAPHIC CREDITS

Front cover: photo © Douglas Friedman, background artwork © de Gournay; p. 4: © Aubrie Pick; pp. 6–7: © Aubrie Pick; p. 8: © Marc-Antoine Coulon; p. 10: © Aubrie Pick; pp. 12–13: © Jeffrey Fulgencio; p. 14: © Jeffrey Fulgencio; p. 16: © Jonathan Rachman; p. 19: © Marc-Antoine Coulon; p. 20: © Jonathan Rachman; p. 22: © Jonathan Rachman; p. 23: © Courtesy of Amanjiwo; p. 24: © Jeffrey Fulgencio; pp. 26–27: © Jonathan Rachman; p. 30: © Jeffrey Fulgencio; p. 32: © Suzanna Scott; pp. 34–36: © Douglas Friedman; p. 37: © Marc-Antoine Coulon; pp. 38–39: © Suzanna Scott; pp. 40–41: © Douglas Friedman; pp. 42–43: © Suzanna Scott; p. 44: © Jeffrey Fulgencio; p. 45: © Douglas Friedman; pp. 46–52: © Douglas Friedman; p. 53: © Marc-Antoine Coulon; pp. 54–55: © Douglas Friedman; pp. 56–71: © Lunghi Media Group; pp. 72–79: © David Duncan Livingston; pp. 80–89: © Christina Cavallaro; pp. 90–101: © Mark Leet; pp. 102–13: © Thayer Allyson Gowdy; p. 114: © John Merkl; pp. 116–18: © David Duncan Livingston; p. 119: © John Merkl; pp. 120–21: © David Duncan Livingston; pp. 122–23: © John Merkl; pp. 124–31: © Aubrie Pick; pp. 132–33: © Drew Altizer; pp. 134–35: © Douglas Friedman; p. 136: © Aubrie Pick; pp. 137–39: © Douglas Friedman; pp. 140–49: © Jeffrey Fulgencio; pp. 150–57: © David Duncan Livingston; pp. 158–69: © Aubrie Pick; pp. 170–85: © Suzanna Scott; p. 186: © Marc-Antoine Coulon; pp. 187–89: © Suzanna Scott; pp. 190–225: © Douglas Friedman; pp. 226–35: © Suzanna Scott; pp. 236–57: © José Manuel Alorda; p. 258: © Audrie Pick; p. 260: © Marc-Antoine Coulon; pp. 262–63: © Douglas Friedman.

ARTISTIC CREDITS

p. 6: © Caroline Lizarraga (hand painted silhouette); pp. 32–45: © de Gournay (wallpaper and mirrors); pp. 34–35: © Boatswain (sconces), © Coup Studio (chair), © Lex Pott (chandelier); p. 36: © L. & J. Lobmeyr (chandelier); pp. 38–39: © Lex Pott (chandelier), © Holly Hunt, (glass side table); pp. 38–43: © Boatswain (sconces), © Coup Studio (chair); pp. 40–43: © Agnes Lloyd-Platt (photographs/Courtesy of Houghton Hall), © Coup Studio (chair), © Konekt (stool); p. 45: © Damian Jones (credenza), © de Gournay (chairs); p. 46: © René Bouché (drawing), © de Gournay (wallpaper); p. 48: © Santiago Parra (abstract painting); p. 50: © Anna Glover (wallpaper); p. 52: © James Goldcrown (abstract art), © Jeremiah Goodman (illustrations); p. 54: © James Goldcrown (abstract art), © Missoni for Stark (carpet); pp. 54–55: © Jeremiah Goodman (illustrations), © Coup Studio (sofa), © Missoni for Stark (carpet); p. 55: © RETNA (abstract painting); p. 64: © Isaac Julien (photograph, right); p. 66: © Zuber (scenic wallpaper); p. 72: © Hahn (original art), © Ironies (chandelier); pp. 75–77: © Hahn (original art); p. 78: © Donghia (mirror); p. 80: © Florian Schneider (backlit art); p. 82: © Holly Hunt (daybed); pp. 82–83: © Donghia (chandelier); p. 84: © Holly Hunt (daybed); p. 86: © Konstantin Bessmertny (painting); p. 87: © Holly Hunt (daybed); p. 102: © Ralph Lauren (lounge chair); p. 134: © Jeremiah Goodman (illustrations); p. 139: © Jeremiah Goodman (illustrations); pp. 140–49: © de Gournay (wallpaper for J. Rachman); p. 155: © Fornasetti for Cole & Son (wallpaper); p. 158: © Nathan Oliveira (painting); p. 160: © Manuel Neri (sculpture); p. 161: © Jean Royère/Adagp, Paris, 2022 (chair); p. 162: © Boris Deutsch (painting); pp. 164–65: © Hahn (original art), © Eero Saarinen (dining table); p. 166: © Le Corbusier/Adagp, Paris, 2022 (painting); p. 168: © Henri Hayden/Adagp, Paris, 2022 (painting); p. 170: © Holly Hunt (table), © Gabriel Scott (chair), © Randal Ford (photograph); p. 172: © Gabriel Scott (pendant and stools); p. 173: © Diane Tate DallasKidd (red wall art), © Aqua Creations (floor lamp), © Zinc (wall coverings); p. 175: © Holly Hunt (chair); pp. 176–77: © Gregorius/Pineo (wallcovering); p. 178: © KGBL (coffee table), © Fisher Weisman (chandelier); pp. 178–79: © Coup Studio (chair and sofa), © de Gournay (wallpaper); pp. 180–81: © Coup Studio (chairs and sofa), © Holly Hunt (table), © Fisher Weisman (chandelier); p. 183: © Ironies (console); p. 188: © Jacques Scandelari (photograph); p. 189–90: © Coup Studio (sofa); p. 190: © Coup Studio (chair); p. 192: © de Gournay (wallpaper); p. 193: © McGuire (stools); pp. 194–95: © Jean Louis Deniot for Baker (sofa, ottoman, and chair), © Fortuny (floor lamp and cushion); p. 198: © Vaughan Lighting (pendant), © Stark Carpet (rug); p. 200: © Ironies (bedside tables); p. 202: © Barbara Barry (desk), © Schumacher (wallpaper); © p. 203: © Arteriors (chandelier), © Bonnie Beauchamp-Cooke (art), © de Gournay (mirror), © Schumacher (wall paper); p. 204: © Marc Chagall/Adagp, Paris, 2022 (paintings) p. 204: © Eduardo Arranz-Bravo/Adagp, Paris, 2022 (painting); p. 206–207: © Estate of Picasso 2022 (painting), © Apparatus (chandelier), © Tod Von Mertens (dining table), © Palecek (dining chairs), © DLV Design (settees), © Bolla, (wing chairs); © Coup Studio (chair), © Stark Carpet (rug); p. 208: © OCHRE (chandelier); p. 209: © Eduardo Arranz-Bravo/Adagp, Paris, 2022 (paintings); p. 210: © Aaron Chang (photograph), © Palecek (dining chairs); pp. 214–15: © Holly Hunt (dining table and chairs); p. 215: © Hahn (original art), © Donghia (table lamp); p. 216: © Stephen De Staebler (sculpture), © Stark Carpet (rug); p. 217: © Jean de Merry (leather wing chair); p. 218: © Gabriel Scott (chandelier); p. 219: © Coup Studio (chair); p. 220: © Flexform (dining chairs); p. 221: © Lindsey Adelman (chandelier); p. 224: © Holly Hunt (daybed); p. 226: © Stark Carpet (rug); p. 228: © Eames (office chair); p. 229: © Stark Carpet (rug); p. 231: © Circa (chandelier); p. 234: © Lee Jofa (wallpaper); p. 235: © de Gournay (wallpaper); p. 236: © Jesus Pedraglio (abstract hanging sculpture), © Stark Carpet (rug); pp. 238–39: © de Gournay (embroidered wallpaper), © Coup Studio (chairs and sofa), © Stark Carpet (rug); p. 240: © de Gournay (wallpaper); p. 241: © Lex Pott (chandelier); pp. 244–45: © Kyle Bunting (area rug); p. 247: © Stark Carpet (rug); p. 249: © Circa (chandelier), © Waterworks (tub and plumbing fixtures); pp. 250–51: © Manuel Canovas (fabric and wallpaper); pp. 252–53: © de Gournay (embroidered wallpaper); p. 254: © Cathrine Raben Davidsen/Adagp, Paris, 2022 (floor lamp); pp. 254–55: © Thibaut (wallpaper and fabric), © Stark Carpet (rug); pp. 256–57: © Dunes and Duchess (chandelier and sconces), © Thibaut (wallpaper and fabric), © Stark Carpet (rug); p. 258: L. & J. Lobmeyr (sconces), © de Gournay (wallpaper).